GEMS

&

GENRES

Painted Wings Publishing

For more information, visit: JHouserWrites.com

Formatting, cover & edge designs by Painted Wings Publishing

Edited by Nia Quinn

ISBNs:

Hardback: 978-1-957334-09-7

Paperback: 978-1-957334-12-7

First Edition: March 2023

10 9 8 7 6 5 4 3 2 1

How to enjoy your gem collection!

-The Display Shelf: Decorate with the top 50 books you read & journaled about. Track your reading stats & fill out your favorites after completing this tome!

-The TBR Pile: 11 pages allow you to easily list 462 books 'To Be Read.'

-Journal Pages: 250 pages have been included to rate & review each book you read. Print off a picture of the cover & secure it in the designated spot, or lean on your artistic skills to recreate it!

-The Dusty DNFs (Did Not Finish): Not every book makes the cut for every reader. 6 pages are included (72 entries) for you to list the title and your progress before you decided to put the book down (e.g. 100/200 pages read, or 50%). A space is included for commentary.

-Extra Pages: 19 extra lined pages have been added in case those included for other topics didn't happen to be enough for your particular reading habits!

-Replacements & Recommendations: Other books & journals offered by the same publisher!

*For best results: use pens, pencils, or markers that are nonbleeding.

**For merch, extra tips, and free templates related to this book journal, go to JHouserWrites.com

Fantasy

Fairy Tales

Romance

Post-Apocalyptic

Literary Fiction

Poetry

Women's Fiction

New Adult

Dystopian

Paranormal

Retellings

Novella

Suspense

Historical Fiction

Science Fiction

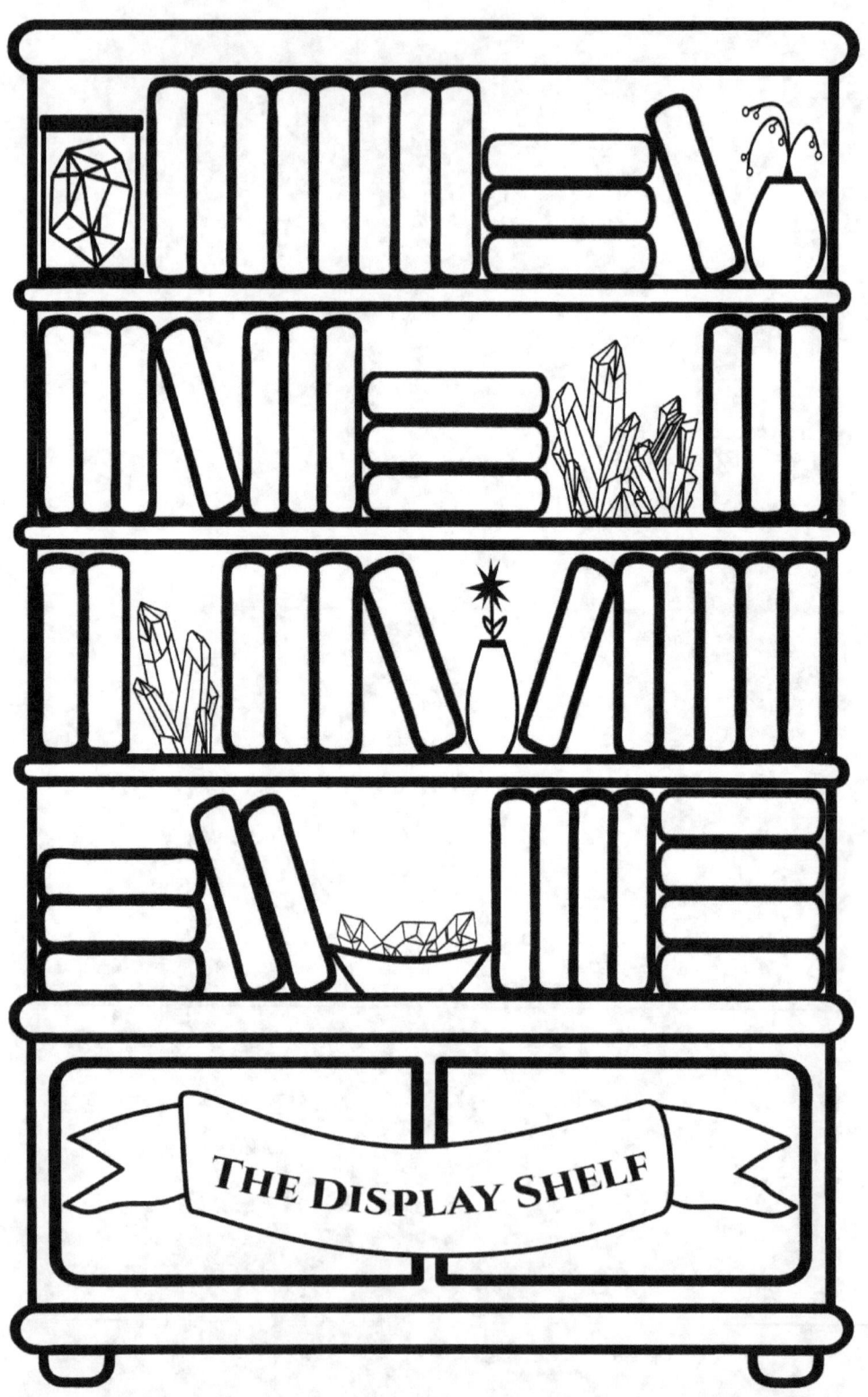

THE DISPLAY SHELF

Favorite Main Characters:

Favorite Side Characters/Love Interests:

Favorite Authors:

Favorite Covers:

The 6 most delectably rereadable

The 3 genres I read the most

My Complete Gem Collection

0   25   50   75   100   125   150   175   200   225   250

Ebook

Print

Audiobook

My Reading Stats

 # * THE GREAT TBR LIST *

 # * THE GREAT TBR LIST *

* The Great TBR List *

 *** THE GREAT TBR LIST ***

 # * THE GREAT TBR LIST *

 # * THE GREAT TBR LIST *

 *** THE GREAT TBR LIST ***

 # * THE GREAT TBR LIST *

 # * THE GREAT TBR LIST *

 # * THE GREAT TBR LIST *

 # * THE GREAT TBR LIST *

TITLE: _____

GENRE: _____

SERIES: _____

AUTHOR: _____

PAGES: _____

STARTED: _____

FINISHED: _____

☆ ☆ ☆ ☆ ☆

FORMAT READ: EBOOK / PRINT / AUDIOBOOK

✓ **SYNOPSIS/THINGS I LIKED:**

_____
_____
_____
_____
_____

🚫 **THINGS I DIDN'T LIKE:**

_____
_____
_____
_____
_____

✏️ **FAVORITE QUOTE(S):**

_____
_____
_____
_____
_____
_____
_____
_____

TITLE: _____

GENRE: _____

SERIES: _____

AUTHOR: _____

PAGES: _____

STARTED: _____

FINISHED: _____

☆☆☆☆☆

FORMAT READ: EBOOK / PRINT / AUDIOBOOK

✓ SYNOPSIS/THINGS I LIKED:

_____
_____
_____
_____

🚫 THINGS I DIDN'T LIKE:

_____
_____
_____
_____
_____

✏️ FAVORITE QUOTE(S):

_____
_____
_____
_____
_____
_____
_____
_____

☑ **SYNOPSIS/THINGS I LIKED:**

_____

_____

_____

_____

_____

🚫 **THINGS I DIDN'T LIKE:**

_____

_____

_____

_____

✏️ **FAVORITE QUOTE(S):**

_____

_____

_____

_____

_____

_____

_____

TITLE: _____

GENRE: _____

SERIES: _____

AUTHOR: _____

PAGES: _____

STARTED: _____

FINISHED: _____

☆ ☆ ☆ ☆ ☆

FORMAT READ: EBOOK / PRINT / AUDIOBOOK **3**

✔ **SYNOPSIS/THINGS I LIKED:**

_____

_____

_____

_____

🚫 **THINGS I DIDN'T LIKE:**

_____

_____

_____

_____

✏️ **FAVORITE QUOTE(S):**

_____

_____

_____

_____

_____

_____

TITLE: _____

GENRE: _____

SERIES: _____

AUTHOR: _____

PAGES: _____

STARTED: _____

FINISHED: _____

☆ ☆ ☆ ☆ ☆

FORMAT READ: EBOOK / PRINT / AUDIOBOOK

4

TITLE: _____

GENRE: _____

SERIES: _____

AUTHOR: _____

PAGES: _____

STARTED: _____

FINISHED: _____

☆ ☆ ☆ ☆ ☆

FORMAT READ: EBOOK / PRINT / AUDIOBOOK

☑ **SYNOPSIS/THINGS I LIKED:**

_____
_____
_____
_____
_____

🚫 **THINGS I DIDN'T LIKE:**

_____
_____
_____
_____
_____

📝 **FAVORITE QUOTE(S):**

_____
_____
_____
_____
_____
_____
_____
_____

TITLE: _____

GENRE: _____

SERIES: _____

AUTHOR: _____

PAGES: _____

STARTED: _____

FINISHED: _____

☆ ☆ ☆ ☆ ☆

FORMAT READ: EBOOK / PRINT / AUDIOBOOK

✓ **SYNOPSIS/THINGS I LIKED:**

_____
_____
_____
_____

🚫 **THINGS I DIDN'T LIKE:**

_____
_____
_____
_____

✎ **FAVORITE QUOTE(S):**

_____
_____
_____
_____
_____
_____

✓ **SYNOPSIS/THINGS I LIKED:**

_____
_____
_____
_____
_____

🚫 **THINGS I DIDN'T LIKE:**

_____
_____
_____
_____

✎ **FAVORITE QUOTE(S):**

_____
_____
_____
_____
_____
_____
_____

TITLE: _____

GENRE: _____

SERIES: _____

AUTHOR: _____

PAGES: _____

STARTED: _____

FINISHED: _____

☆ ☆ ☆ ☆ ☆

FORMAT READ: EBOOK / PRINT / AUDIOBOOK

✓ SYNOPSIS/THINGS I LIKED:

_____

_____

_____

_____

🚫 THINGS I DIDN'T LIKE:

_____

_____

_____

_____

📝 FAVORITE QUOTE(S):

_____

_____

_____

_____

_____

_____

_____

TITLE: _____

GENRE: _____

SERIES: _____

AUTHOR: _____

PAGES: _____

STARTED: _____

FINISHED: _____

☆ ☆ ☆ ☆ ☆

FORMAT READ: EBOOK / PRINT / AUDIOBOOK

8

TITLE: _____

GENRE: _____

SERIES: _____

AUTHOR: _____

PAGES: _____

STARTED: _____

FINISHED: _____

☆ ☆ ☆ ☆ ☆

FORMAT READ: EBOOK / PRINT / AUDIOBOOK

✓ **SYNOPSIS/THINGS I LIKED:** _____
_____
_____
_____
_____

🚫 **THINGS I DIDN'T LIKE:** _____
_____
_____
_____
_____

✎ **FAVORITE QUOTE(S):** _____
_____
_____
_____
_____
_____
_____
_____

TITLE: _____

GENRE: _____

SERIES: _____

AUTHOR: _____

PAGES: _____

STARTED: _____

FINISHED: _____

☆ ☆ ☆ ☆ ☆

FORMAT READ: EBOOK / PRINT / AUDIOBOOK

✓ **SYNOPSIS/THINGS I LIKED:**

_____
_____
_____
_____

🚫 **THINGS I DIDN'T LIKE:**

_____
_____
_____
_____

✍ **FAVORITE QUOTE(S):**

_____
_____
_____
_____
_____
_____

☑ Synopsis/Things I liked:

_____
_____
_____
_____
_____

🚫 Things I didn't like:

_____
_____
_____
_____
_____

✏ Favorite quote(s):

_____
_____
_____
_____
_____
_____

Title: _____

Genre: _____

Series: _____

Author: _____

Pages: _____

Started: _____

Finished: _____

☆ ☆ ☆ ☆ ☆

✓ **SYNOPSIS/THINGS I LIKED:**

_____

_____

_____

_____

_____

🚫 **THINGS I DIDN'T LIKE:**

_____

_____

_____

_____

_____

✎ **FAVORITE QUOTE(S):**

_____

_____

_____

_____

_____

_____

_____

TITLE: _____

GENRE: _____

SERIES: _____

AUTHOR: _____

PAGES: _____

STARTED: _____

FINISHED: _____

☆☆☆☆☆

FORMAT READ: EBOOK / PRINT / AUDIOBOOK

TITLE: _____

GENRE: _____

SERIES: _____

AUTHOR: _____

PAGES: _____

STARTED: _____

FINISHED: _____

☆☆☆☆☆

FORMAT READ: EBOOK / PRINT / AUDIOBOOK

✓ **SYNOPSIS/THINGS I LIKED:**

_____

_____

_____

_____

_____

🚫 **THINGS I DIDN'T LIKE:**

_____

_____

_____

_____

_____

✏️ **FAVORITE QUOTE(S):**

_____

_____

_____

_____

_____

_____

_____

TITLE: _____

GENRE: _____

SERIES: _____

AUTHOR: _____

PAGES: _____

STARTED: _____

FINISHED: _____

☆ ☆ ☆ ☆ ☆

FORMAT READ: EBOOK / PRINT / AUDIOBOOK

✓ **SYNOPSIS/THINGS I LIKED:**

_____
_____
_____
_____
_____

🚫 **THINGS I DIDN'T LIKE:**

_____
_____
_____
_____
_____

✎ **FAVORITE QUOTE(S):**

_____
_____
_____
_____
_____
_____
_____

✔ **SYNOPSIS/THINGS I LIKED:**

_____
_____
_____
_____
_____

🚫 **THINGS I DIDN'T LIKE:**

_____
_____
_____
_____

✎ **FAVORITE QUOTE(S):**

_____
_____
_____
_____
_____
_____
_____

TITLE: _____

GENRE: _____

SERIES: _____

AUTHOR: _____

PAGES: _____

STARTED: _____

FINISHED: _____

☆ ☆ ☆ ☆ ☆

✓ **SYNOPSIS/THINGS I LIKED:**

_____
_____
_____
_____
_____

🚫 **THINGS I DIDN'T LIKE:**

_____
_____
_____
_____
_____

✎ **FAVORITE QUOTE(S):**

_____
_____
_____
_____
_____
_____
_____

TITLE: _____

GENRE: _____

SERIES: _____

AUTHOR: _____

PAGES: _____

STARTED: _____

FINISHED: _____

☆ ☆ ☆ ☆ ☆

FORMAT READ: EBOOK / PRINT / AUDIOBOOK

TITLE: _____

GENRE: _____

SERIES: _____

AUTHOR: _____

PAGES: _____

STARTED: _____

FINISHED: _____

☆☆☆☆☆

FORMAT READ: EBOOK / PRINT / AUDIOBOOK

✔ **SYNOPSIS/THINGS I LIKED:**

_____
_____
_____
_____
_____

🚫 **THINGS I DIDN'T LIKE:**

_____
_____
_____
_____
_____

✎ **FAVORITE QUOTE(S):**

_____
_____
_____
_____
_____
_____
_____

TITLE: _____

GENRE: _____

SERIES: _____

AUTHOR: _____

PAGES: _____

STARTED: _____

FINISHED: _____

☆ ☆ ☆ ☆ ☆

FORMAT READ: EBOOK / PRINT / AUDIOBOOK

✓ SYNOPSIS/THINGS I LIKED:
_____
_____
_____
_____

🚫 THINGS I DIDN'T LIKE:
_____
_____
_____
_____

✎ FAVORITE QUOTE(S):
_____
_____
_____
_____
_____
_____

✓ **SYNOPSIS/THINGS I LIKED:**

_____
_____
_____
_____
_____

🚫 **THINGS I DIDN'T LIKE:**

_____
_____
_____
_____

✎ **FAVORITE QUOTE(S):**

_____
_____
_____
_____
_____
_____

TITLE: _____

GENRE: _____

SERIES: _____

AUTHOR: _____

PAGES: _____

STARTED: _____

FINISHED: _____

☆ ☆ ☆ ☆ ☆

FORMAT READ: EBOOK / PRINT / AUDIOBOOK 19

✓ **SYNOPSIS/THINGS I LIKED:**

_____
_____
_____
_____
_____

🚫 **THINGS I DIDN'T LIKE:**

_____
_____
_____
_____
_____

✏️ **FAVORITE QUOTE(S):**

_____
_____
_____
_____
_____
_____
_____

TITLE: _____

GENRE: _____

SERIES: _____

AUTHOR: _____

PAGES: _____

STARTED: _____

FINISHED: _____

☆ ☆ ☆ ☆ ☆

FORMAT READ: EBOOK / PRINT / AUDIOBOOK

TITLE: _____

GENRE: _____

SERIES: _____

AUTHOR: _____

PAGES: _____

STARTED: _____

FINISHED: _____

☆ ☆ ☆ ☆ ☆

FORMAT READ: EBOOK / PRINT / AUDIOBOOK

✓ **SYNOPSIS/THINGS I LIKED:**

_____
_____
_____
_____

🚫 **THINGS I DIDN'T LIKE:**

_____
_____
_____
_____

✍ **FAVORITE QUOTE(S):**

_____
_____
_____
_____
_____
_____

TITLE: _____

GENRE: _____

SERIES: _____

AUTHOR: _____

PAGES: _____

STARTED: _____

FINISHED: _____

☆ ☆ ☆ ☆ ☆

FORMAT READ: EBOOK / PRINT / AUDIOBOOK

✔ **SYNOPSIS/THINGS I LIKED:** _____

_____

_____

_____

_____

🚫 **THINGS I DIDN'T LIKE:** _____

_____

_____

_____

_____

✏ **FAVORITE QUOTE(S):** _____

_____

_____

_____

_____

_____

_____

✔ **SYNOPSIS/THINGS I LIKED:**

_____
_____
_____
_____
_____

🚫 **THINGS I DIDN'T LIKE:**

_____
_____
_____
_____

✎ **FAVORITE QUOTE(S):**

_____
_____
_____
_____
_____
_____

TITLE: _____

GENRE: _____

SERIES: _____

AUTHOR: _____

PAGES: _____

STARTED: _____

FINISHED: _____

☆ ☆ ☆ ☆ ☆

FORMAT READ: EBOOK / PRINT / AUDIOBOOK **23**

☑ SYNOPSIS/THINGS I LIKED:

_____

_____

_____

_____

🚫 THINGS I DIDN'T LIKE:

_____

_____

_____

_____

✎ FAVORITE QUOTE(S):

_____

_____

_____

_____

_____

_____

_____

TITLE: _____

GENRE: _____

SERIES: _____

AUTHOR: _____

PAGES: _____

STARTED: _____

FINISHED: _____

☆ ☆ ☆ ☆ ☆

FORMAT READ: EBOOK / PRINT / AUDIOBOOK

TITLE: _____

GENRE: _____

SERIES: _____

AUTHOR: _____

PAGES: _____

STARTED: _____

FINISHED: _____

☆☆☆☆☆

FORMAT READ: EBOOK / PRINT / AUDIOBOOK

☑ **SYNOPSIS/THINGS I LIKED:**

_____
_____
_____
_____

🚫 **THINGS I DIDN'T LIKE:**

_____
_____
_____
_____

✎ **FAVORITE QUOTE(S):**

_____
_____
_____
_____
_____
_____
_____

TITLE: _____

GENRE: _____

SERIES: _____

AUTHOR: _____

PAGES: _____

STARTED: _____

FINISHED: _____

☆ ☆ ☆ ☆ ☆

FORMAT READ: EBOOK / PRINT / AUDIOBOOK

✔ SYNOPSIS/THINGS I LIKED:

_____

_____

_____

_____

_____

🚫 THINGS I DIDN'T LIKE:

_____

_____

_____

_____

_____

✏ FAVORITE QUOTE(S):

_____

_____

_____

_____

_____

_____

_____

✔️ **SYNOPSIS/THINGS I LIKED:**

_____

_____

_____

_____

🚫 **THINGS I DIDN'T LIKE:**

_____

_____

_____

_____

✏️ **FAVORITE QUOTE(S):**

_____

_____

_____

_____

_____

_____

TITLE: _____

GENRE: _____

SERIES: _____

AUTHOR: _____

PAGES: _____

STARTED: _____

FINISHED: _____

☆ ☆ ☆ ☆ ☆

✅ **SYNOPSIS/THINGS I LIKED:**

_____
_____
_____
_____

🚫 **THINGS I DIDN'T LIKE:**

_____
_____
_____
_____

✏️ **FAVORITE QUOTE(S):**

_____
_____
_____
_____
_____
_____

TITLE: _____

GENRE: _____

SERIES: _____

AUTHOR: _____

PAGES: _____

STARTED: _____

FINISHED: _____

☆ ☆ ☆ ☆ ☆

FORMAT READ: EBOOK / PRINT / AUDIOBOOK

TITLE: _____

GENRE: _____

SERIES: _____

AUTHOR: _____

PAGES: _____

STARTED: _____

FINISHED: _____

☆☆☆☆☆

FORMAT READ: EBOOK / PRINT / AUDIOBOOK

✓ **SYNOPSIS/THINGS I LIKED:**

_____
_____
_____
_____
_____

🚫 **THINGS I DIDN'T LIKE:**

_____
_____
_____
_____
_____

✏️ **FAVORITE QUOTE(S):**

_____
_____
_____
_____
_____
_____
_____

TITLE: _____

GENRE: _____

SERIES: _____

AUTHOR: _____

PAGES: _____

STARTED: _____

FINISHED: _____

☆☆☆☆☆

FORMAT READ: EBOOK / PRINT / AUDIOBOOK

✔ **SYNOPSIS/THINGS I LIKED:**

_____
_____
_____
_____
_____

🚫 **THINGS I DIDN'T LIKE:**

_____
_____
_____
_____
_____

✎ **FAVORITE QUOTE(S):**

_____
_____
_____
_____
_____
_____
_____

☑ **SYNOPSIS/THINGS I LIKED:**

_____

_____

_____

_____

_____

🚫 **THINGS I DIDN'T LIKE:**

_____

_____

_____

_____

✎ **FAVORITE QUOTE(S):**

_____

_____

_____

_____

_____

_____

_____

TITLE: _____

GENRE: _____

SERIES: _____

AUTHOR: _____

PAGES: _____

STARTED: _____

FINISHED: _____

☆ ☆ ☆ ☆ ☆

✓ **SYNOPSIS/THINGS I LIKED:**

_____

_____

_____

_____

_____

🚫 **THINGS I DIDN'T LIKE:**

_____

_____

_____

_____

_____

✒ **FAVORITE QUOTE(S):**

_____

_____

_____

_____

_____

_____

_____

TITLE: _____

GENRE: _____

SERIES: _____

AUTHOR: _____

PAGES: _____

STARTED: _____

FINISHED: _____

☆ ☆ ☆ ☆ ☆

FORMAT READ: EBOOK / PRINT / AUDIOBOOK

TITLE: _____

GENRE: _____

SERIES: _____

AUTHOR: _____

PAGES: _____

STARTED: _____

FINISHED: _____

☆☆☆☆☆

FORMAT READ: EBOOK / PRINT / AUDIOBOOK

✓ SYNOPSIS/THINGS I LIKED:

_____
_____
_____
_____

🚫 THINGS I DIDN'T LIKE:

_____
_____
_____
_____

✒ FAVORITE QUOTE(S):

_____
_____
_____
_____
_____
_____
_____

TITLE: _____

GENRE: _____

SERIES: _____

AUTHOR: _____

PAGES: _____

STARTED: _____

FINISHED: _____

☆ ☆ ☆ ☆ ☆

FORMAT READ: EBOOK / PRINT / AUDIOBOOK

✓ **SYNOPSIS/THINGS I LIKED:**

_____
_____
_____
_____

🚫 **THINGS I DIDN'T LIKE:**

_____
_____
_____
_____

📝 **FAVORITE QUOTE(S):**

_____
_____
_____
_____
_____
_____

✓ **SYNOPSIS/THINGS I LIKED:**

_____
_____
_____
_____

🚫 **THINGS I DIDN'T LIKE:**

_____
_____
_____
_____

✏️ **FAVORITE QUOTE(S):**

_____
_____
_____
_____
_____
_____

TITLE: _____

GENRE: _____

SERIES: _____

AUTHOR: _____

PAGES: _____

STARTED: _____

FINISHED: _____

☆ ☆ ☆ ☆ ☆

✓ **SYNOPSIS/THINGS I LIKED:**

_____

_____

_____

_____

🚫 **THINGS I DIDN'T LIKE:**

_____

_____

_____

_____

✎ **FAVORITE QUOTE(S):**

_____

_____

_____

_____

_____

_____

_____

TITLE: _____

GENRE: _____

SERIES: _____

AUTHOR: _____

PAGES: _____

STARTED: _____

FINISHED: _____

☆ ☆ ☆ ☆ ☆

FORMAT READ: EBOOK / PRINT / AUDIOBOOK

TITLE: _____

GENRE: _____

SERIES: _____

AUTHOR: _____

PAGES: _____

STARTED: _____

FINISHED: _____

☆ ☆ ☆ ☆ ☆

FORMAT READ: EBOOK / PRINT / AUDIOBOOK

✓ **SYNOPSIS/THINGS I LIKED:**

_____
_____
_____
_____
_____

🚫 **THINGS I DIDN'T LIKE:**

_____
_____
_____
_____
_____

✎ **FAVORITE QUOTE(S):**

_____
_____
_____
_____
_____
_____
_____
_____

TITLE: _____

GENRE: _____

SERIES: _____

AUTHOR: _____

PAGES: _____

STARTED: _____

FINISHED: _____

☆ ☆ ☆ ☆ ☆

FORMAT READ: EBOOK / PRINT / AUDIOBOOK

✓ **SYNOPSIS/THINGS I LIKED:**

_____

_____

_____

_____

🚫 **THINGS I DIDN'T LIKE:**

_____

_____

_____

_____

✏️ **FAVORITE QUOTE(S):**

_____

_____

_____

_____

_____

_____

_____

☑ **SYNOPSIS/THINGS I LIKED:**

_____
_____
_____
_____
_____

🚫 **THINGS I DIDN'T LIKE:**

_____
_____
_____
_____

✎ **FAVORITE QUOTE(S):**

_____
_____
_____
_____
_____
_____
_____

TITLE: _____

GENRE: _____

SERIES: _____

AUTHOR: _____

PAGES: _____

STARTED: _____

FINISHED: _____

☆ ☆ ☆ ☆ ☆

☑ **SYNOPSIS/THINGS I LIKED:**

_____
_____
_____
_____

🚫 **THINGS I DIDN'T LIKE:**

_____
_____
_____
_____

✎ **FAVORITE QUOTE(S):**

_____
_____
_____
_____
_____
_____
_____

TITLE: _____

GENRE: _____

SERIES: _____

AUTHOR: _____

PAGES: _____

STARTED: _____

FINISHED: _____

☆ ☆ ☆ ☆ ☆

FORMAT READ: EBOOK / PRINT / AUDIOBOOK

TITLE: _____

GENRE: _____

SERIES: _____

AUTHOR: _____

PAGES: _____

STARTED: _____

FINISHED: _____

☆☆☆☆☆

FORMAT READ: EBOOK / PRINT / AUDIOBOOK

✔ **SYNOPSIS/THINGS I LIKED:**

_____
_____
_____
_____
_____

🚫 **THINGS I DIDN'T LIKE:**

_____
_____
_____
_____
_____

✎ **FAVORITE QUOTE(S):**

_____
_____
_____
_____
_____
_____
_____
_____

TITLE: _____

GENRE: _____

SERIES: _____

AUTHOR: _____

PAGES: _____

STARTED: _____

FINISHED: _____

☆ ☆ ☆ ☆ ☆

FORMAT READ: EBOOK / PRINT / AUDIOBOOK

☑ **SYNOPSIS/THINGS I LIKED:**

_____
_____
_____
_____

🚫 **THINGS I DIDN'T LIKE:**

_____
_____
_____
_____

✎ **FAVORITE QUOTE(S):**

_____
_____
_____
_____
_____
_____

☑ **SYNOPSIS/THINGS I LIKED:**

_____

_____

_____

_____

_____

🚫 **THINGS I DIDN'T LIKE:**

_____

_____

_____

_____

✎ **FAVORITE QUOTE(S):**

_____

_____

_____

_____

_____

_____

TITLE: _____

GENRE: _____

SERIES: _____

AUTHOR: _____

PAGES: _____

STARTED: _____

FINISHED: _____

☆☆☆☆☆

✔ **SYNOPSIS/THINGS I LIKED:**

_____
_____
_____
_____
_____

🚫 **THINGS I DIDN'T LIKE:**

_____
_____
_____
_____
_____

✎ **FAVORITE QUOTE(S):**

_____
_____
_____
_____
_____
_____
_____

TITLE: _____

GENRE: _____

SERIES: _____

AUTHOR: _____

PAGES: _____

STARTED: _____

FINISHED: _____

☆ ☆ ☆ ☆ ☆

FORMAT READ: EBOOK / PRINT / AUDIOBOOK

TITLE: _____

GENRE: _____

SERIES: _____

AUTHOR: _____

PAGES: _____

STARTED: _____

FINISHED: _____

☆ ☆ ☆ ☆ ☆

FORMAT READ: EBOOK / PRINT / AUDIOBOOK

☑ **SYNOPSIS/THINGS I LIKED:**

_____
_____
_____
_____
_____

🚫 **THINGS I DIDN'T LIKE:**

_____
_____
_____
_____
_____

🖊 **FAVORITE QUOTE(S):**

_____
_____
_____
_____
_____
_____
_____

TITLE: _____

GENRE: _____

SERIES: _____

AUTHOR: _____

PAGES: _____

STARTED: _____

FINISHED: _____

☆☆☆☆☆

FORMAT READ: EBOOK / PRINT / AUDIOBOOK

✓ **SYNOPSIS/THINGS I LIKED:**

_____
_____
_____
_____

🚫 **THINGS I DIDN'T LIKE:**

_____
_____
_____
_____

📝 **FAVORITE QUOTE(S):**

_____
_____
_____
_____
_____
_____

✓ **SYNOPSIS/THINGS I LIKED:**

_____

_____

_____

_____

🚫 **THINGS I DIDN'T LIKE:**

_____

_____

_____

_____

✎ **FAVORITE QUOTE(S):**

_____

_____

_____

_____

_____

_____

TITLE: _____

GENRE: _____

SERIES: _____

AUTHOR: _____

PAGES: _____

STARTED: _____

FINISHED: _____

☆ ☆ ☆ ☆ ☆

✅ **SYNOPSIS/THINGS I LIKED:**

_____

_____

_____

_____

🚫 **THINGS I DIDN'T LIKE:**

_____

_____

_____

_____

✏️ **FAVORITE QUOTE(S):**

_____

_____

_____

_____

_____

_____

TITLE: _____

GENRE: _____

SERIES: _____

AUTHOR: _____

PAGES: _____

STARTED: _____

FINISHED: _____

☆ ☆ ☆ ☆ ☆

FORMAT READ: EBOOK / PRINT / AUDIOBOOK

TITLE: _____

GENRE: _____

SERIES: _____

AUTHOR: _____

PAGES: _____

STARTED: _____

FINISHED: _____

☆ ☆ ☆ ☆ ☆

FORMAT READ: EBOOK / PRINT / AUDIOBOOK

✓ **SYNOPSIS/THINGS I LIKED:**

_____

_____

_____

_____

_____

🚫 **THINGS I DIDN'T LIKE:**

_____

_____

_____

_____

_____

✎ **FAVORITE QUOTE(S):**

_____

_____

_____

_____

_____

_____

_____

_____

TITLE: _____

GENRE: _____

SERIES: _____

AUTHOR: _____

PAGES: _____

STARTED: _____

FINISHED: _____

☆ ☆ ☆ ☆ ☆

FORMAT READ: EBOOK / PRINT / AUDIOBOOK

☑ **SYNOPSIS/THINGS I LIKED:**

_____
_____
_____
_____
_____

🚫 **THINGS I DIDN'T LIKE:**

_____
_____
_____
_____
_____

✎ **FAVORITE QUOTE(S):**

_____
_____
_____
_____
_____
_____
_____

✅ **SYNOPSIS/THINGS I LIKED:**

_____

_____

_____

_____

_____

🚫 **THINGS I DIDN'T LIKE:**

_____

_____

_____

_____

✏️ **FAVORITE QUOTE(S):**

_____

_____

_____

_____

_____

_____

_____

TITLE: _____

GENRE: _____

SERIES: _____

AUTHOR: _____

PAGES: _____

STARTED: _____

FINISHED: _____

☆ ☆ ☆ ☆ ☆

✓ SYNOPSIS/THINGS I LIKED:

_____

_____

_____

_____

🚫 THINGS I DIDN'T LIKE:

_____

_____

_____

_____

✎ FAVORITE QUOTE(S):

_____

_____

_____

_____

_____

_____

TITLE: _____

GENRE: _____

SERIES: _____

AUTHOR: _____

PAGES: _____

STARTED: _____

FINISHED: _____

☆ ☆ ☆ ☆ ☆

FORMAT READ: EBOOK / PRINT / AUDIOBOOK

TITLE: _____

GENRE: _____

SERIES: _____

AUTHOR: _____

PAGES: _____

STARTED: _____

FINISHED: _____

☆ ☆ ☆ ☆ ☆

FORMAT READ: EBOOK / PRINT / AUDIOBOOK

☑ **SYNOPSIS/THINGS I LIKED:** _____

_____

_____

_____

_____

_____

🚫 **THINGS I DIDN'T LIKE:** _____

_____

_____

_____

_____

_____

✎ **FAVORITE QUOTE(S):** _____

_____

_____

_____

_____

_____

_____

_____

TITLE: _____

GENRE: _____

SERIES: _____

AUTHOR: _____

PAGES: _____

STARTED: _____

FINISHED: _____

☆ ☆ ☆ ☆ ☆

FORMAT READ: EBOOK / PRINT / AUDIOBOOK

✓ **SYNOPSIS/THINGS I LIKED:**

_____
_____
_____
_____
_____

🚫 **THINGS I DIDN'T LIKE:**

_____
_____
_____
_____
_____

✎ **FAVORITE QUOTE(S):**

_____
_____
_____
_____
_____
_____
_____

✅ **SYNOPSIS/THINGS I LIKED:**

_____

_____

_____

_____

_____

🚫 **THINGS I DIDN'T LIKE:**

_____

_____

_____

_____

✏️ **FAVORITE QUOTE(S):**

_____

_____

_____

_____

_____

_____

TITLE: _____

GENRE: _____

SERIES: _____

AUTHOR: _____

PAGES: _____

STARTED: _____

FINISHED: _____

☆ ☆ ☆ ☆ ☆

✔ **SYNOPSIS/THINGS I LIKED:**

_____

_____

_____

_____

🚫 **THINGS I DIDN'T LIKE:**

_____

_____

_____

_____

✏ **FAVORITE QUOTE(S):**

_____

_____

_____

_____

_____

_____

TITLE: _____

GENRE: _____

SERIES: _____

AUTHOR: _____

PAGES: _____

STARTED: _____

FINISHED: _____

☆ ☆ ☆ ☆ ☆

FORMAT READ: EBOOK / PRINT / AUDIOBOOK

TITLE: _____

GENRE: _____

SERIES: _____

AUTHOR: _____

PAGES: _____

STARTED: _____

FINISHED: _____

☆ ☆ ☆ ☆ ☆

FORMAT READ: EBOOK / PRINT / AUDIOBOOK

✓ **SYNOPSIS/THINGS I LIKED:**

_____
_____
_____
_____
_____

🚫 **THINGS I DIDN'T LIKE:**

_____
_____
_____
_____
_____

✎ **FAVORITE QUOTE(S):**

_____
_____
_____
_____
_____
_____
_____

TITLE: _____

GENRE: _____

SERIES: _____

AUTHOR: _____

PAGES: _____

STARTED: _____

FINISHED: _____

☆☆☆☆☆

FORMAT READ: EBOOK / PRINT / AUDIOBOOK

✓ **SYNOPSIS/THINGS I LIKED:**

_____
_____
_____
_____
_____

🚫 **THINGS I DIDN'T LIKE:**

_____
_____
_____
_____
_____

✎ **FAVORITE QUOTE(S):**

_____
_____
_____
_____
_____
_____
_____

☑ **SYNOPSIS/THINGS I LIKED:**

_____
_____
_____
_____

🚫 **THINGS I DIDN'T LIKE:**

_____
_____
_____
_____

📝 **FAVORITE QUOTE(S):**

_____
_____
_____
_____
_____

TITLE: _____

GENRE: _____

SERIES: _____

AUTHOR: _____

PAGES: _____

STARTED: _____

FINISHED: _____

☆ ☆ ☆ ☆ ☆

✔ **SYNOPSIS/THINGS I LIKED:**

_____
_____
_____
_____
_____

🚫 **THINGS I DIDN'T LIKE:**

_____
_____
_____
_____

✎ **FAVORITE QUOTE(S):**

_____
_____
_____
_____
_____
_____

TITLE: _____

GENRE: _____

SERIES: _____

AUTHOR: _____

PAGES: _____

STARTED: _____

FINISHED: _____

☆ ☆ ☆ ☆ ☆

FORMAT READ: EBOOK / PRINT / AUDIOBOOK

TITLE: _____

GENRE: _____

SERIES: _____

AUTHOR: _____

PAGES: _____

STARTED: _____

FINISHED: _____

☆ ☆ ☆ ☆ ☆

FORMAT READ: EBOOK / PRINT / AUDIOBOOK

✔ **SYNOPSIS/THINGS I LIKED:**
_____
_____
_____
_____
_____

🚫 **THINGS I DIDN'T LIKE:**
_____
_____
_____
_____
_____

✏ **FAVORITE QUOTE(S):**
_____
_____
_____
_____
_____
_____
_____
_____

TITLE: _____

GENRE: _____

SERIES: _____

AUTHOR: _____

PAGES: _____

STARTED: _____

FINISHED: _____

☆☆☆☆☆

FORMAT READ: EBOOK / PRINT / AUDIOBOOK

✓ **SYNOPSIS/THINGS I LIKED:**

_____
_____
_____
_____
_____

🚫 **THINGS I DIDN'T LIKE:**

_____
_____
_____
_____
_____

✏️ **FAVORITE QUOTE(S):**

_____
_____
_____
_____
_____
_____
_____

✅ **Synopsis/Things I liked:**

_____

_____

_____

_____

🚫 **Things I didn't like:**

_____

_____

_____

_____

✏️ **Favorite quote(s):**

_____

_____

_____

_____

_____

_____

Title: _____

Genre: _____

Series: _____

Author: _____

Pages: _____

Started: _____

Finished: _____

☆ ☆ ☆ ☆ ☆

Format read: Ebook / Print / Audiobook 63

✓ **SYNOPSIS/THINGS I LIKED:**

_____

_____

_____

_____

_____

🚫 **THINGS I DIDN'T LIKE:**

_____

_____

_____

_____

_____

✏️ **FAVORITE QUOTE(S):**

_____

_____

_____

_____

_____

_____

TITLE: _____

GENRE: _____

SERIES: _____

AUTHOR: _____

PAGES: _____

STARTED: _____

FINISHED: _____

☆ ☆ ☆ ☆ ☆

FORMAT READ: EBOOK / PRINT / AUDIOBOOK

TITLE: _____

GENRE: _____

SERIES: _____

AUTHOR: _____

PAGES: _____

STARTED: _____

FINISHED: _____

☆☆☆☆☆

FORMAT READ: EBOOK / PRINT / AUDIOBOOK

✓ SYNOPSIS/THINGS I LIKED: _____

_____

_____

_____

_____

🚫 THINGS I DIDN'T LIKE: _____

_____

_____

_____

_____

✎ FAVORITE QUOTE(S): _____

_____

_____

_____

_____

_____

_____

_____

TITLE: _____

GENRE: _____

SERIES: _____

AUTHOR: _____

PAGES: _____

STARTED: _____

FINISHED: _____

☆ ☆ ☆ ☆ ☆

FORMAT READ: EBOOK / PRINT / AUDIOBOOK

☑ **SYNOPSIS/THINGS I LIKED:**

_____
_____
_____
_____

🚫 **THINGS I DIDN'T LIKE:**

_____
_____
_____
_____

✒ **FAVORITE QUOTE(S):**

_____
_____
_____
_____
_____
_____
_____

☑ **SYNOPSIS/THINGS I LIKED:**

_____
_____
_____
_____

🚫 **THINGS I DIDN'T LIKE:**

_____
_____
_____
_____

✏️ **FAVORITE QUOTE(S):**

_____
_____
_____
_____
_____
_____

TITLE: _____

GENRE: _____

SERIES: _____

AUTHOR: _____

PAGES: _____

STARTED: _____

FINISHED: _____

☆ ☆ ☆ ☆ ☆

✔ SYNOPSIS/THINGS I LIKED:

_____

_____

_____

_____

🚫 THINGS I DIDN'T LIKE:

_____

_____

_____

_____

✎ FAVORITE QUOTE(S):

_____

_____

_____

_____

_____

_____

TITLE: _____

GENRE: _____

SERIES: _____

AUTHOR: _____

PAGES: _____

STARTED: _____

FINISHED: _____

☆ ☆ ☆ ☆ ☆

FORMAT READ: EBOOK / PRINT / AUDIOBOOK

TITLE: _____

GENRE: _____

SERIES: _____

AUTHOR: _____

PAGES: _____

STARTED: _____

FINISHED: _____

☆ ☆ ☆ ☆ ☆

FORMAT READ: EBOOK / PRINT / AUDIOBOOK

✓ **SYNOPSIS/THINGS I LIKED:**

_____
_____
_____
_____

🚫 **THINGS I DIDN'T LIKE:**

_____
_____
_____
_____

✏️ **FAVORITE QUOTE(S):**

_____
_____
_____
_____
_____
_____
_____

TITLE: _____

GENRE: _____

SERIES: _____

AUTHOR: _____

PAGES: _____

STARTED: _____

FINISHED: _____

☆ ☆ ☆ ☆ ☆

FORMAT READ: EBOOK / PRINT / AUDIOBOOK

☑ SYNOPSIS/THINGS I LIKED:

_____
_____
_____
_____
_____

🚫 THINGS I DIDN'T LIKE:

_____
_____
_____
_____

✍ FAVORITE QUOTE(S):

_____
_____
_____
_____
_____
_____
_____

✓ **Synopsis/Things I liked:**

_____
_____
_____
_____

🚫 **Things I didn't like:**

_____
_____
_____
_____

✏️ **Favorite quote(s):**

_____
_____
_____
_____
_____
_____

Title: _____

Genre: _____

Series: _____

Author: _____

Pages: _____

Started: _____

Finished: _____

☆ ☆ ☆ ☆ ☆

✓ **SYNOPSIS/THINGS I LIKED:**

_____

_____

_____

_____

🚫 **THINGS I DIDN'T LIKE:**

_____

_____

_____

_____

✎ **FAVORITE QUOTE(S):**

_____

_____

_____

_____

_____

_____

TITLE: _____

GENRE: _____

SERIES: _____

AUTHOR: _____

PAGES: _____

STARTED: _____

FINISHED: _____

☆ ☆ ☆ ☆ ☆

FORMAT READ: EBOOK / PRINT / AUDIOBOOK

TITLE: _____

GENRE: _____

SERIES: _____

AUTHOR: _____

PAGES: _____

STARTED: _____

FINISHED: _____

☆☆☆☆☆

FORMAT READ: EBOOK / PRINT / AUDIOBOOK

✓ SYNOPSIS/THINGS I LIKED:
_____
_____
_____
_____

🚫 THINGS I DIDN'T LIKE:
_____
_____
_____
_____

✎ FAVORITE QUOTE(S):
_____
_____
_____
_____
_____
_____
_____

TITLE: _____

GENRE: _____

SERIES: _____

AUTHOR: _____

PAGES: _____

STARTED: _____

FINISHED: _____

☆ ☆ ☆ ☆ ☆

FORMAT READ: EBOOK / PRINT / AUDIOBOOK

✔ **SYNOPSIS/THINGS I LIKED:**

_____
_____
_____
_____
_____

🚫 **THINGS I DIDN'T LIKE:**

_____
_____
_____
_____
_____

✎ **FAVORITE QUOTE(S):**

_____
_____
_____
_____
_____
_____
_____
_____

✅ **SYNOPSIS/THINGS I LIKED:**

_____

_____

_____

_____

🚫 **THINGS I DIDN'T LIKE:**

_____

_____

_____

_____

📝 **FAVORITE QUOTE(S):**

_____

_____

_____

_____

_____

_____

TITLE: _____

GENRE: _____

SERIES: _____

AUTHOR: _____

PAGES: _____

STARTED: _____

FINISHED: _____

☆☆☆☆☆

FORMAT READ: EBOOK / PRINT / AUDIOBOOK **75**

✓ **SYNOPSIS/THINGS I LIKED:**

_____

_____

_____

_____

_____

🚫 **THINGS I DIDN'T LIKE:**

_____

_____

_____

_____

✏️ **FAVORITE QUOTE(S):**

_____

_____

_____

_____

_____

_____

TITLE: _____

GENRE: _____

SERIES: _____

AUTHOR: _____

PAGES: _____

STARTED: _____

FINISHED: _____

☆ ☆ ☆ ☆ ☆

FORMAT READ: EBOOK / PRINT / AUDIOBOOK

TITLE: _____

GENRE: _____

SERIES: _____

AUTHOR: _____

PAGES: _____

STARTED: _____

FINISHED: _____

☆ ☆ ☆ ☆ ☆

FORMAT READ: EBOOK / PRINT / AUDIOBOOK

✓ **SYNOPSIS/THINGS I LIKED:**

_____
_____
_____
_____
_____

🚫 **THINGS I DIDN'T LIKE:**

_____
_____
_____
_____
_____

✏️ **FAVORITE QUOTE(S):**

_____
_____
_____
_____
_____
_____
_____

TITLE: _____

GENRE: _____

SERIES: _____

AUTHOR: _____

PAGES: _____

STARTED: _____

FINISHED: _____

☆☆☆☆☆

FORMAT READ: EBOOK / PRINT / AUDIOBOOK

☑ **SYNOPSIS/THINGS I LIKED:**

_____
_____
_____
_____

🚫 **THINGS I DIDN'T LIKE:**

_____
_____
_____
_____

✎ **FAVORITE QUOTE(S):**

_____
_____
_____
_____
_____
_____
_____

✓ **SYNOPSIS/THINGS I LIKED:**

_____

_____

_____

_____

🚫 **THINGS I DIDN'T LIKE:**

_____

_____

_____

_____

✏️ **FAVORITE QUOTE(S):**

_____

_____

_____

_____

_____

_____

TITLE: _____

GENRE: _____

SERIES: _____

AUTHOR: _____

PAGES: _____

STARTED: _____

FINISHED: _____

☆ ☆ ☆ ☆ ☆

✓ SYNOPSIS/THINGS I LIKED:
_____
_____
_____
_____

🚫 THINGS I DIDN'T LIKE:
_____
_____
_____
_____
_____

✎ FAVORITE QUOTE(S):
_____
_____
_____
_____
_____
_____

TITLE: _____

GENRE: _____

SERIES: _____

AUTHOR: _____

PAGES: _____

STARTED: _____

FINISHED: _____

☆ ☆ ☆ ☆ ☆

FORMAT READ: EBOOK / PRINT / AUDIOBOOK

TITLE: _____

GENRE: _____

SERIES: _____

AUTHOR: _____

PAGES: _____

STARTED: _____

FINISHED: _____

☆ ☆ ☆ ☆ ☆

FORMAT READ: EBOOK / PRINT / AUDIOBOOK

✓ **SYNOPSIS/THINGS I LIKED:**

_____
_____
_____
_____
_____

🚫 **THINGS I DIDN'T LIKE:**

_____
_____
_____
_____
_____

✏️ **FAVORITE QUOTE(S):**

_____
_____
_____
_____
_____
_____
_____
_____

TITLE: _____

GENRE: _____

SERIES: _____

AUTHOR: _____

PAGES: _____

STARTED: _____

FINISHED: _____

☆ ☆ ☆ ☆ ☆

FORMAT READ: EBOOK / PRINT / AUDIOBOOK

✓ **SYNOPSIS/THINGS I LIKED:**

_____

_____

_____

_____

🚫 **THINGS I DIDN'T LIKE:**

_____

_____

_____

_____

✒ **FAVORITE QUOTE(S):**

_____

_____

_____

_____

_____

_____

☑ **Synopsis/Things I liked:**

_____
_____
_____
_____

🚫 **Things I didn't like:**

_____
_____
_____
_____

✎ **Favorite quote(s):**

_____
_____
_____
_____
_____
_____

Title: _____

Genre: _____

Series: _____

Author: _____

Pages: _____

Started: _____

Finished: _____

☆☆☆☆☆

☑ **SYNOPSIS/THINGS I LIKED:**

_____
_____
_____
_____
_____

🚫 **THINGS I DIDN'T LIKE:**

_____
_____
_____
_____
_____

✎ **FAVORITE QUOTE(S):**

_____
_____
_____
_____
_____
_____
_____

TITLE: _____

GENRE: _____

SERIES: _____

AUTHOR: _____

PAGES: _____

STARTED: _____

FINISHED: _____

☆ ☆ ☆ ☆ ☆

FORMAT READ: EBOOK / PRINT / AUDIOBOOK

TITLE: _____

GENRE: _____

SERIES: _____

AUTHOR: _____

PAGES: _____

STARTED: _____

FINISHED: _____

☆ ☆ ☆ ☆ ☆

FORMAT READ: EBOOK / PRINT / AUDIOBOOK

✓ **SYNOPSIS/THINGS I LIKED:**

_____

_____

_____

_____

🚫 **THINGS I DIDN'T LIKE:**

_____

_____

_____

_____

✎ **FAVORITE QUOTE(S):**

_____

_____

_____

_____

_____

_____

TITLE: _____

GENRE: _____

SERIES: _____

AUTHOR: _____

PAGES: _____

STARTED: _____

FINISHED: _____

☆ ☆ ☆ ☆ ☆

FORMAT READ: EBOOK / PRINT / AUDIOBOOK

✔ **SYNOPSIS/THINGS I LIKED:**

_____
_____
_____
_____

🚫 **THINGS I DIDN'T LIKE:**

_____
_____
_____
_____

✎ **FAVORITE QUOTE(S):**

_____
_____
_____
_____
_____
_____
_____

✓ **SYNOPSIS/THINGS I LIKED:**

_____

_____

_____

_____

_____

🚫 **THINGS I DIDN'T LIKE:**

_____

_____

_____

_____

✎ **FAVORITE QUOTE(S):**

_____

_____

_____

_____

_____

_____

_____

TITLE: _____

GENRE: _____

SERIES: _____

AUTHOR: _____

PAGES: _____

STARTED: _____

FINISHED: _____

☆ ☆ ☆ ☆ ☆

✓ **SYNOPSIS/THINGS I LIKED:**

_____
_____
_____
_____

🚫 **THINGS I DIDN'T LIKE:**

_____
_____
_____
_____

✎ **FAVORITE QUOTE(S):**

_____
_____
_____
_____
_____
_____

TITLE: _____

GENRE: _____

SERIES: _____

AUTHOR: _____

PAGES: _____

STARTED: _____

FINISHED: _____

☆ ☆ ☆ ☆ ☆

FORMAT READ: EBOOK / PRINT / AUDIOBOOK

TITLE: _____

GENRE: _____

SERIES: _____

AUTHOR: _____

PAGES: _____

STARTED: _____

FINISHED: _____

☆ ☆ ☆ ☆ ☆

FORMAT READ: EBOOK / PRINT / AUDIOBOOK

✓ **SYNOPSIS/THINGS I LIKED:**

_____
_____
_____
_____
_____

🚫 **THINGS I DIDN'T LIKE:**

_____
_____
_____
_____
_____

✏️ **FAVORITE QUOTE(S):**

_____
_____
_____
_____
_____
_____
_____

TITLE: _____

GENRE: _____

SERIES: _____

AUTHOR: _____

PAGES: _____

STARTED: _____

FINISHED: _____

☆☆☆☆☆

FORMAT READ: EBOOK / PRINT / AUDIOBOOK

☑ **SYNOPSIS/THINGS I LIKED:**

_____
_____
_____
_____

🚫 **THINGS I DIDN'T LIKE:**

_____
_____
_____
_____

✎ **FAVORITE QUOTE(S):**

_____
_____
_____
_____
_____
_____
_____

✓ **SYNOPSIS/THINGS I LIKED:**

_____

_____

_____

_____

_____

🚫 **THINGS I DIDN'T LIKE:**

_____

_____

_____

_____

_____

✏️ **FAVORITE QUOTE(S):**

_____

_____

_____

_____

_____

_____

TITLE: _____

GENRE: _____

SERIES: _____

AUTHOR: _____

PAGES: _____

STARTED: _____

FINISHED: _____

☆ ☆ ☆ ☆ ☆

FORMAT READ: EBOOK / PRINT / AUDIOBOOK 91

✓ **SYNOPSIS/THINGS I LIKED:**

_____
_____
_____
_____
_____

🚫 **THINGS I DIDN'T LIKE:**

_____
_____
_____
_____
_____

✏️ **FAVORITE QUOTE(S):**

_____
_____
_____
_____
_____
_____
_____

TITLE: _____

GENRE: _____

SERIES: _____

AUTHOR: _____

PAGES: _____

STARTED: _____

FINISHED: _____

☆ ☆ ☆ ☆ ☆

FORMAT READ: EBOOK / PRINT / AUDIOBOOK

TITLE: _____

GENRE: _____

SERIES: _____

AUTHOR: _____

PAGES: _____

STARTED: _____

FINISHED: _____

☆ ☆ ☆ ☆ ☆

FORMAT READ: EBOOK / PRINT / AUDIOBOOK

✓ SYNOPSIS/THINGS I LIKED:
_____
_____
_____
_____
_____

🚫 THINGS I DIDN'T LIKE:
_____
_____
_____
_____
_____

✎ FAVORITE QUOTE(S):
_____
_____
_____
_____
_____
_____
_____

TITLE: _____

GENRE: _____

SERIES: _____

AUTHOR: _____

PAGES: _____

STARTED: _____

FINISHED: _____

☆☆☆☆☆

FORMAT READ: EBOOK / PRINT / AUDIOBOOK

✓ **SYNOPSIS/THINGS I LIKED:**

_____
_____
_____
_____

🚫 **THINGS I DIDN'T LIKE:**

_____
_____
_____
_____
_____

✍ **FAVORITE QUOTE(S):**

_____
_____
_____
_____
_____
_____
_____

✔️ **SYNOPSIS/THINGS I LIKED:**

_____
_____
_____
_____
_____

🚫 **THINGS I DIDN'T LIKE:**

_____
_____
_____
_____

✏️ **FAVORITE QUOTE(S):**

_____
_____
_____
_____
_____
_____

TITLE: _____

GENRE: _____

SERIES: _____

AUTHOR: _____

PAGES: _____

STARTED: _____

FINISHED: _____

☆ ☆ ☆ ☆ ☆

✓ Synopsis/Things I liked:

_____

_____

_____

_____

🚫 Things I didn't like:

_____

_____

_____

_____

✐ Favorite quote(s):

_____

_____

_____

_____

_____

_____

_____

Title: _____

Genre: _____

Series: _____

Author: _____

Pages: _____

Started: _____

Finished: _____

☆ ☆ ☆ ☆ ☆

Format read: Ebook / Print / Audiobook

TITLE: _____

GENRE: _____

SERIES: _____

AUTHOR: _____

PAGES: _____

STARTED: _____

FINISHED: _____

☆ ☆ ☆ ☆ ☆

FORMAT READ: EBOOK / PRINT / AUDIOBOOK

✓ **SYNOPSIS/THINGS I LIKED:**

_____
_____
_____
_____

🚫 **THINGS I DIDN'T LIKE:**

_____
_____
_____
_____

✎ **FAVORITE QUOTE(S):**

_____
_____
_____
_____
_____
_____
_____

TITLE: _____

GENRE: _____

SERIES: _____

AUTHOR: _____

PAGES: _____

STARTED: _____

FINISHED: _____

☆☆☆☆☆

FORMAT READ: EBOOK / PRINT / AUDIOBOOK

✓ **SYNOPSIS/THINGS I LIKED:**

_____
_____
_____
_____
_____

🚫 **THINGS I DIDN'T LIKE:**

_____
_____
_____
_____
_____

✎ **FAVORITE QUOTE(S):**

_____
_____
_____
_____
_____
_____
_____
_____

✔ SYNOPSIS/THINGS I LIKED:

_____

_____

_____

_____

🚫 THINGS I DIDN'T LIKE:

_____

_____

_____

_____

✎ FAVORITE QUOTE(S):

_____

_____

_____

_____

_____

_____

TITLE: _____

GENRE: _____

SERIES: _____

AUTHOR: _____

PAGES: _____

STARTED: _____

FINISHED: _____

☆ ☆ ☆ ☆ ☆

FORMAT READ: EBOOK / PRINT / AUDIOBOOK **99**

✓ **SYNOPSIS/THINGS I LIKED:**

_____

_____

_____

_____

🚫 **THINGS I DIDN'T LIKE:**

_____

_____

_____

_____

✏️ **FAVORITE QUOTE(S):**

_____

_____

_____

_____

_____

_____

TITLE: _____

GENRE: _____

SERIES: _____

AUTHOR: _____

PAGES: _____

STARTED: _____

FINISHED: _____

☆ ☆ ☆ ☆ ☆

FORMAT READ: EBOOK / PRINT / AUDIOBOOK

TITLE:

GENRE:

SERIES:

AUTHOR:

PAGES:

STARTED:

FINISHED:

☆ ☆ ☆ ☆ ☆

FORMAT READ: EBOOK / PRINT / AUDIOBOOK

✓ **SYNOPSIS/THINGS I LIKED:**

🚫 **THINGS I DIDN'T LIKE:**

✏️ **FAVORITE QUOTE(S):**

TITLE: _____

GENRE: _____

SERIES: _____

AUTHOR: _____

PAGES: _____

STARTED: _____

FINISHED: _____

☆ ☆ ☆ ☆ ☆

FORMAT READ: EBOOK / PRINT / AUDIOBOOK

✓ **SYNOPSIS/THINGS I LIKED:**

_____
_____
_____
_____

🚫 **THINGS I DIDN'T LIKE:**

_____
_____
_____
_____

✎ **FAVORITE QUOTE(S):**

_____
_____
_____
_____
_____
_____

✓ **SYNOPSIS/THINGS I LIKED:**

_____
_____
_____
_____
_____

🚫 **THINGS I DIDN'T LIKE:**

_____
_____
_____
_____
_____

📝 **FAVORITE QUOTE(S):**

_____
_____
_____
_____
_____
_____

TITLE: _____

GENRE: _____

SERIES: _____

AUTHOR: _____

PAGES: _____

STARTED: _____

FINISHED: _____

☆ ☆ ☆ ☆ ☆

FORMAT READ: EBOOK / PRINT / AUDIOBOOK

✓ **SYNOPSIS/THINGS I LIKED:**

_____

_____

_____

_____

🚫 **THINGS I DIDN'T LIKE:**

_____

_____

_____

_____

✎ **FAVORITE QUOTE(S):**

_____

_____

_____

_____

_____

TITLE: _____

GENRE: _____

SERIES: _____

AUTHOR: _____

PAGES: _____

STARTED: _____

FINISHED: _____

☆ ☆ ☆ ☆ ☆

FORMAT READ: EBOOK / PRINT / AUDIOBOOK

TITLE: _____

GENRE: _____

SERIES: _____

AUTHOR: _____

PAGES: _____

STARTED: _____

FINISHED: _____

☆ ☆ ☆ ☆ ☆

FORMAT READ: EBOOK / PRINT / AUDIOBOOK

✔ **SYNOPSIS/THINGS I LIKED:**

_____
_____
_____
_____

🚫 **THINGS I DIDN'T LIKE:**

_____
_____
_____
_____

📝 **FAVORITE QUOTE(S):**

_____
_____
_____
_____
_____
_____
_____

TITLE: _____

GENRE: _____

SERIES: _____

AUTHOR: _____

PAGES: _____

STARTED: _____

FINISHED: _____

☆☆☆☆☆

FORMAT READ: EBOOK / PRINT / AUDIOBOOK

✓ **SYNOPSIS/THINGS I LIKED:**

_____
_____
_____
_____

🚫 **THINGS I DIDN'T LIKE:**

_____
_____
_____
_____
_____

✒ **FAVORITE QUOTE(S):**

_____
_____
_____
_____
_____
_____
_____

✔️ **SYNOPSIS/THINGS I LIKED:**

_____
_____
_____
_____

🚫 **THINGS I DIDN'T LIKE:**

_____
_____
_____
_____
_____

✏️ **FAVORITE QUOTE(S):**

_____
_____
_____
_____
_____
_____

TITLE: _____

GENRE: _____

SERIES: _____

AUTHOR: _____

PAGES: _____

STARTED: _____

FINISHED: _____

☆ ☆ ☆ ☆ ☆

FORMAT READ: EBOOK / PRINT / AUDIOBOOK

✓ **SYNOPSIS/THINGS I LIKED:**

_____

_____

_____

_____

🚫 **THINGS I DIDN'T LIKE:**

_____

_____

_____

_____

✎ **FAVORITE QUOTE(S):**

_____

_____

_____

_____

_____

_____

TITLE: _____

GENRE: _____

SERIES: _____

AUTHOR: _____

PAGES: _____

STARTED: _____

FINISHED: _____

☆ ☆ ☆ ☆ ☆

FORMAT READ: EBOOK / PRINT / AUDIOBOOK

TITLE: _____

GENRE: _____

SERIES: _____

AUTHOR: _____

PAGES: _____

STARTED: _____

FINISHED: _____

☆ ☆ ☆ ☆ ☆

FORMAT READ: EBOOK / PRINT / AUDIOBOOK

✓ **SYNOPSIS/THINGS I LIKED:**

_____
_____
_____
_____
_____

🚫 **THINGS I DIDN'T LIKE:**

_____
_____
_____
_____
_____

✎ **FAVORITE QUOTE(S):**

_____
_____
_____
_____
_____
_____
_____

TITLE: _____

GENRE: _____

SERIES: _____

AUTHOR: _____

PAGES: _____

STARTED: _____

FINISHED: _____

☆☆☆☆☆

FORMAT READ: EBOOK / PRINT / AUDIOBOOK

✔️ **SYNOPSIS/THINGS I LIKED:**

_____
_____
_____
_____

🚫 **THINGS I DIDN'T LIKE:**

_____
_____
_____
_____

✒️ **FAVORITE QUOTE(S):**

_____
_____
_____
_____
_____
_____
_____

✓ **SYNOPSIS/THINGS I LIKED:**

_____

_____

_____

_____

🚫 **THINGS I DIDN'T LIKE:**

_____

_____

_____

_____

✏️ **FAVORITE QUOTE(S):**

_____

_____

_____

_____

_____

_____

TITLE: _____

GENRE: _____

SERIES: _____

AUTHOR: _____

PAGES: _____

STARTED: _____

FINISHED: _____

☆ ☆ ☆ ☆ ☆

FORMAT READ: EBOOK / PRINT / AUDIOBOOK

☑ **Synopsis/Things I liked:**

_____

_____

_____

_____

🚫 **Things I didn't like:**

_____

_____

_____

_____

📝 **Favorite quote(s):**

_____

_____

_____

_____

_____

_____

Title: _____

Genre: _____

Series: _____

Author: _____

Pages: _____

Started: _____

Finished: _____

☆ ☆ ☆ ☆ ☆

Format read: Ebook / Print / Audiobook

TITLE: _____

GENRE: _____

SERIES: _____

AUTHOR: _____

PAGES: _____

STARTED: _____

FINISHED: _____

☆ ☆ ☆ ☆ ☆

FORMAT READ: EBOOK / PRINT / AUDIOBOOK

☑ **SYNOPSIS/THINGS I LIKED:**

_____
_____
_____
_____

🚫 **THINGS I DIDN'T LIKE:**

_____
_____
_____
_____

✒ **FAVORITE QUOTE(S):**

_____
_____
_____
_____
_____
_____
_____

TITLE: _____

GENRE: _____

SERIES: _____

AUTHOR: _____

PAGES: _____

STARTED: _____

FINISHED: _____

☆ ☆ ☆ ☆ ☆

FORMAT READ: EBOOK / PRINT / AUDIOBOOK

✓ **SYNOPSIS/THINGS I LIKED:**

_____
_____
_____
_____
_____

🚫 **THINGS I DIDN'T LIKE:**

_____
_____
_____
_____
_____

✏️ **FAVORITE QUOTE(S):**

_____
_____
_____
_____
_____
_____
_____

✔️ **Synopsis/Things I liked:**

_____

_____

_____

_____

🚫 **Things I didn't like:**

_____

_____

_____

_____

✏️ **Favorite quote(s):**

_____

_____

_____

_____

_____

Title: _____

Genre: _____

Series: _____

Author: _____

Pages: _____

Started: _____

Finished: _____

☆ ☆ ☆ ☆ ☆

Format read: Ebook / Print / Audiobook

✓ **SYNOPSIS/THINGS I LIKED:**

_____
_____
_____
_____

🚫 **THINGS I DIDN'T LIKE:**

_____
_____
_____
_____

✎ **FAVORITE QUOTE(S):**

_____
_____
_____
_____
_____
_____

TITLE: _____

GENRE: _____

SERIES: _____

AUTHOR: _____

PAGES: _____

STARTED: _____

FINISHED: _____

☆ ☆ ☆ ☆ ☆

FORMAT READ: EBOOK / PRINT / AUDIOBOOK

TITLE: _____

GENRE: _____

SERIES: _____

AUTHOR: _____

PAGES: _____

STARTED: _____

FINISHED: _____

☆ ☆ ☆ ☆ ☆

FORMAT READ: EBOOK / PRINT / AUDIOBOOK

✓ **SYNOPSIS/THINGS I LIKED:**

_____
_____
_____
_____

🚫 **THINGS I DIDN'T LIKE:**

_____
_____
_____
_____

📝 **FAVORITE QUOTE(S):**

_____
_____
_____
_____
_____
_____
_____

TITLE: _____

GENRE: _____

SERIES: _____

AUTHOR: _____

PAGES: _____

STARTED: _____

FINISHED: _____

☆ ☆ ☆ ☆ ☆

FORMAT READ: EBOOK / PRINT / AUDIOBOOK

✓ **SYNOPSIS/THINGS I LIKED:**

_____
_____
_____
_____

🚫 **THINGS I DIDN'T LIKE:**

_____
_____
_____
_____

📝 **FAVORITE QUOTE(S):**

_____
_____
_____
_____
_____
_____

✔ **Synopsis/Things I liked:**

_____
_____
_____
_____

🚫 **Things I didn't like:**

_____
_____
_____
_____

✎ **Favorite quote(s):**

_____
_____
_____
_____
_____
_____

Title: _____

Genre: _____

Series: _____

Author: _____

Pages: _____

Started: _____

Finished: _____

☆ ☆ ☆ ☆ ☆

Format read: Ebook / Print / Audiobook

✔ **SYNOPSIS/THINGS I LIKED:**

_____
_____
_____
_____

🚫 **THINGS I DIDN'T LIKE:**

_____
_____
_____
_____

✏️ **FAVORITE QUOTE(S):**

_____
_____
_____
_____
_____
_____

TITLE: _____

GENRE: _____

SERIES: _____

AUTHOR: _____

PAGES: _____

STARTED: _____

FINISHED: _____

☆ ☆ ☆ ☆ ☆

FORMAT READ: EBOOK / PRINT / AUDIOBOOK

Title: _____

Genre: _____

Series: _____

Author: _____

Pages: _____

Started: _____

Finished: _____

☆☆☆☆☆

FORMAT READ: EBOOK / PRINT / AUDIOBOOK

✓ **Synopsis/Things I liked:**

_____
_____
_____
_____

🚫 **Things I didn't like:**

_____
_____
_____
_____

✎ **Favorite quote(s):**

_____
_____
_____
_____
_____
_____
_____

TITLE: _____

GENRE: _____

SERIES: _____

AUTHOR: _____

PAGES: _____

STARTED: _____

FINISHED: _____

☆ ☆ ☆ ☆ ☆

FORMAT READ: EBOOK / PRINT / AUDIOBOOK

✓ **SYNOPSIS/THINGS I LIKED:**

_____
_____
_____
_____

🚫 **THINGS I DIDN'T LIKE:**

_____
_____
_____
_____

✎ **FAVORITE QUOTE(S):**

_____
_____
_____
_____
_____
_____

✓ **SYNOPSIS/THINGS I LIKED:**

_____
_____
_____
_____

🚫 **THINGS I DIDN'T LIKE:**

_____
_____
_____
_____

✎ **FAVORITE QUOTE(S):**

_____
_____
_____
_____
_____
_____
_____

TITLE: _____

GENRE: _____

SERIES: _____

AUTHOR: _____

PAGES: _____

STARTED: _____

FINISHED: _____

☆ ☆ ☆ ☆ ☆

FORMAT READ: EBOOK / PRINT / AUDIOBOOK

✔ **SYNOPSIS/THINGS I LIKED:**

_____
_____
_____
_____

🚫 **THINGS I DIDN'T LIKE:**

_____
_____
_____
_____
_____

✎ **FAVORITE QUOTE(S):**

_____
_____
_____
_____
_____
_____

TITLE: _____

GENRE: _____

SERIES: _____

AUTHOR: _____

PAGES: _____

STARTED: _____

FINISHED: _____

☆ ☆ ☆ ☆ ☆

FORMAT READ: EBOOK / PRINT / AUDIOBOOK

TITLE: _____

GENRE: _____

SERIES: _____

AUTHOR: _____

PAGES: _____

STARTED: _____

FINISHED: _____

☆ ☆ ☆ ☆ ☆

FORMAT READ: EBOOK / PRINT / AUDIOBOOK

✔ **SYNOPSIS/THINGS I LIKED:**

_____
_____
_____
_____
_____

🚫 **THINGS I DIDN'T LIKE:**

_____
_____
_____
_____
_____

✏️ **FAVORITE QUOTE(S):**

_____
_____
_____
_____
_____
_____
_____

TITLE: _____

GENRE: _____

SERIES: _____

AUTHOR: _____

PAGES: _____

STARTED: _____

FINISHED: _____

☆ ☆ ☆ ☆ ☆

FORMAT READ: EBOOK / PRINT / AUDIOBOOK

✓ **SYNOPSIS/THINGS I LIKED:**

_____
_____
_____
_____
_____

🚫 **THINGS I DIDN'T LIKE:**

_____
_____
_____
_____
_____

📝 **FAVORITE QUOTE(S):**

_____
_____
_____
_____
_____
_____
_____
_____

✓ **SYNOPSIS/THINGS I LIKED:**

_____

_____

_____

_____

🚫 **THINGS I DIDN'T LIKE:**

_____

_____

_____

_____

✎ **FAVORITE QUOTE(S):**

_____

_____

_____

_____

_____

_____

TITLE: _____

GENRE: _____

SERIES: _____

AUTHOR: _____

PAGES: _____

STARTED: _____

FINISHED: _____

☆ ☆ ☆ ☆ ☆

FORMAT READ: EBOOK / PRINT / AUDIOBOOK

✓ **SYNOPSIS/THINGS I LIKED:**

_____
_____
_____
_____

🚫 **THINGS I DIDN'T LIKE:**

_____
_____
_____
_____

🖊 **FAVORITE QUOTE(S):**

_____
_____
_____
_____
_____
_____

TITLE: _____

GENRE: _____

SERIES: _____

AUTHOR: _____

PAGES: _____

STARTED: _____

FINISHED: _____

☆ ☆ ☆ ☆ ☆

FORMAT READ: EBOOK / PRINT / AUDIOBOOK

TITLE: _____

GENRE: _____

SERIES: _____

AUTHOR: _____

PAGES: _____

STARTED: _____

FINISHED: _____

☆ ☆ ☆ ☆ ☆

FORMAT READ: EBOOK / PRINT / AUDIOBOOK

✓ **SYNOPSIS/THINGS I LIKED:**

_____
_____
_____
_____

🚫 **THINGS I DIDN'T LIKE:**

_____
_____
_____
_____

✏️ **FAVORITE QUOTE(S):**

_____
_____
_____
_____
_____
_____
_____

TITLE: _____

GENRE: _____

SERIES: _____

AUTHOR: _____

PAGES: _____

STARTED: _____

FINISHED: _____

☆ ☆ ☆ ☆ ☆

FORMAT READ: EBOOK / PRINT / AUDIOBOOK

✓ **SYNOPSIS/THINGS I LIKED:**

_____
_____
_____
_____

🚫 **THINGS I DIDN'T LIKE:**

_____
_____
_____
_____

✎ **FAVORITE QUOTE(S):**

_____
_____
_____
_____
_____
_____

✔️ **SYNOPSIS/THINGS I LIKED:**

_____

_____

_____

_____

🚫 **THINGS I DIDN'T LIKE:**

_____

_____

_____

_____

✏️ **FAVORITE QUOTE(S):**

_____

_____

_____

_____

_____

_____

TITLE: _____

GENRE: _____

SERIES: _____

AUTHOR: _____

PAGES: _____

STARTED: _____

FINISHED: _____

☆ ☆ ☆ ☆ ☆

FORMAT READ: EBOOK / PRINT / AUDIOBOOK

✔ **SYNOPSIS/THINGS I LIKED:**

_____

_____

_____

_____

🚫 **THINGS I DIDN'T LIKE:**

_____

_____

_____

_____

✏ **FAVORITE QUOTE(S):**

_____

_____

_____

_____

_____

_____

TITLE: _____

GENRE: _____

SERIES: _____

AUTHOR: _____

PAGES: _____

STARTED: _____

FINISHED: _____

☆ ☆ ☆ ☆ ☆

FORMAT READ: EBOOK / PRINT / AUDIOBOOK

TITLE: _____

GENRE: _____

SERIES: _____

AUTHOR: _____

PAGES: _____

STARTED: _____

FINISHED: _____

☆ ☆ ☆ ☆ ☆

FORMAT READ: EBOOK / PRINT / AUDIOBOOK

✓ **SYNOPSIS/THINGS I LIKED:**

_____
_____
_____
_____
_____

🚫 **THINGS I DIDN'T LIKE:**

_____
_____
_____
_____
_____

✎ **FAVORITE QUOTE(S):**

_____
_____
_____
_____
_____
_____
_____
_____

TITLE: _____

GENRE: _____

SERIES: _____

AUTHOR: _____

PAGES: _____

STARTED: _____

FINISHED: _____

☆☆☆☆☆

FORMAT READ: EBOOK / PRINT / AUDIOBOOK

✓ **SYNOPSIS/THINGS I LIKED:**

_____
_____
_____
_____

🚫 **THINGS I DIDN'T LIKE:**

_____
_____
_____
_____

✒ **FAVORITE QUOTE(S):**

_____
_____
_____
_____
_____
_____

✔ **SYNOPSIS/THINGS I LIKED:**

_____

_____

_____

_____

🚫 **THINGS I DIDN'T LIKE:**

_____

_____

_____

_____

✏ **FAVORITE QUOTE(S):**

_____

_____

_____

_____

_____

_____

TITLE: _____

GENRE: _____

SERIES: _____

AUTHOR: _____

PAGES: _____

STARTED: _____

FINISHED: _____

☆ ☆ ☆ ☆ ☆

FORMAT READ: EBOOK / PRINT / AUDIOBOOK

✅ **Synopsis/Things I liked:**

_____

_____

_____

_____

🚫 **Things I didn't like:**

_____

_____

_____

_____

📝 **Favorite quote(s):**

_____

_____

_____

_____

_____

Title: _____

Genre: _____

Series: _____

Author: _____

Pages: _____

Started: _____

Finished: _____

☆ ☆ ☆ ☆ ☆

Format read: Ebook / Print / Audiobook

TITLE: _____

GENRE: _____

SERIES: _____

AUTHOR: _____

PAGES: _____

STARTED: _____

FINISHED: _____

☆ ☆ ☆ ☆ ☆

FORMAT READ: EBOOK / PRINT / AUDIOBOOK

✓ **SYNOPSIS/THINGS I LIKED:**

_____
_____
_____
_____
_____

🚫 **THINGS I DIDN'T LIKE:**

_____
_____
_____
_____
_____

✎ **FAVORITE QUOTE(S):**

_____
_____
_____
_____
_____
_____
_____
_____

TITLE: _____

GENRE: _____

SERIES: _____

AUTHOR: _____

PAGES: _____

STARTED: _____

FINISHED: _____

☆ ☆ ☆ ☆ ☆

FORMAT READ: EBOOK / PRINT / AUDIOBOOK

✓ **SYNOPSIS/THINGS I LIKED:**

_____
_____
_____
_____

🚫 **THINGS I DIDN'T LIKE:**

_____
_____
_____
_____

✏️ **FAVORITE QUOTE(S):**

_____
_____
_____
_____
_____
_____
_____

☑ **SYNOPSIS/THINGS I LIKED:**

_____

_____

_____

_____

🚫 **THINGS I DIDN'T LIKE:**

_____

_____

_____

_____

_____

📝 **FAVORITE QUOTE(S):**

_____

_____

_____

_____

_____

_____

TITLE: _____

GENRE: _____

SERIES: _____

AUTHOR: _____

PAGES: _____

STARTED: _____

FINISHED: _____

☆ ☆ ☆ ☆ ☆

FORMAT READ: EBOOK / PRINT / AUDIOBOOK

☑ **SYNOPSIS/THINGS I LIKED:**

_____

_____

_____

_____

🚫 **THINGS I DIDN'T LIKE:**

_____

_____

_____

_____

📝 **FAVORITE QUOTE(S):**

_____

_____

_____

_____

_____

_____

TITLE: _____

GENRE: _____

SERIES: _____

AUTHOR: _____

PAGES: _____

STARTED: _____

FINISHED: _____

☆ ☆ ☆ ☆ ☆

FORMAT READ: EBOOK / PRINT / AUDIOBOOK

TITLE: _____

GENRE: _____

SERIES: _____

AUTHOR: _____

PAGES: _____

STARTED: _____

FINISHED: _____

☆ ☆ ☆ ☆ ☆

FORMAT READ: EBOOK / PRINT / AUDIOBOOK

✔ SYNOPSIS/THINGS I LIKED:

_____
_____
_____
_____

🚫 THINGS I DIDN'T LIKE:

_____
_____
_____
_____

✎ FAVORITE QUOTE(S):

_____
_____
_____
_____
_____
_____
_____

TITLE: _____

GENRE: _____

SERIES: _____

AUTHOR: _____

PAGES: _____

STARTED: _____

FINISHED: _____

☆ ☆ ☆ ☆ ☆

FORMAT READ: EBOOK / PRINT / AUDIOBOOK

✓ **SYNOPSIS/THINGS I LIKED:**

_____
_____
_____
_____

🚫 **THINGS I DIDN'T LIKE:**

_____
_____
_____
_____

✎ **FAVORITE QUOTE(S):**

_____
_____
_____
_____
_____
_____
_____

☑ **SYNOPSIS/THINGS I LIKED:**

_____
_____
_____
_____

🚫 **THINGS I DIDN'T LIKE:**

_____
_____
_____
_____

✎ **FAVORITE QUOTE(S):**

_____
_____
_____
_____
_____
_____

TITLE: _____

GENRE: _____

SERIES: _____

AUTHOR: _____

PAGES: _____

STARTED: _____

FINISHED: _____

☆☆☆☆☆

FORMAT READ: EBOOK / PRINT / AUDIOBOOK

✅ **SYNOPSIS/THINGS I LIKED:**

_____

_____

_____

_____

🚫 **THINGS I DIDN'T LIKE:**

_____

_____

_____

_____

✏️ **FAVORITE QUOTE(S):**

_____

_____

_____

_____

_____

_____

TITLE: _____

GENRE: _____

SERIES: _____

AUTHOR: _____

PAGES: _____

STARTED: _____

FINISHED: _____

⭐ ⭐ ⭐ ⭐ ⭐

FORMAT READ: EBOOK / PRINT / AUDIOBOOK

TITLE: _____

GENRE: _____

SERIES: _____

AUTHOR: _____

PAGES: _____

STARTED: _____

FINISHED: _____

☆ ☆ ☆ ☆ ☆

FORMAT READ: EBOOK / PRINT / AUDIOBOOK

✓ **SYNOPSIS/THINGS I LIKED:**

_____
_____
_____
_____

🚫 **THINGS I DIDN'T LIKE:**

_____
_____
_____
_____

✒ **FAVORITE QUOTE(S):**

_____
_____
_____
_____
_____
_____
_____

TITLE: _____

GENRE: _____

SERIES: _____

AUTHOR: _____

PAGES: _____

STARTED: _____

FINISHED: _____

☆☆☆☆☆

FORMAT READ: EBOOK / PRINT / AUDIOBOOK

✔️ **SYNOPSIS/THINGS I LIKED:**

_____
_____
_____
_____

🚫 **THINGS I DIDN'T LIKE:**

_____
_____
_____
_____

✎ **FAVORITE QUOTE(S):**

_____
_____
_____
_____
_____
_____

✔ **SYNOPSIS/THINGS I LIKED:**

_____

_____

_____

_____

🚫 **THINGS I DIDN'T LIKE:**

_____

_____

_____

_____

📝 **FAVORITE QUOTE(S):**

_____

_____

_____

_____

_____

_____

TITLE: _____

GENRE: _____

SERIES: _____

AUTHOR: _____

PAGES: _____

STARTED: _____

FINISHED: _____

☆ ☆ ☆ ☆ ☆

FORMAT READ: EBOOK / PRINT / AUDIOBOOK

✓ **SYNOPSIS/THINGS I LIKED:**

_____

_____

_____

_____

🚫 **THINGS I DIDN'T LIKE:**

_____

_____

_____

_____

✎ **FAVORITE QUOTE(S):**

_____

_____

_____

_____

_____

_____

TITLE: _____

GENRE: _____

SERIES: _____

AUTHOR: _____

PAGES: _____

STARTED: _____

FINISHED: _____

☆ ☆ ☆ ☆ ☆

FORMAT READ: EBOOK / PRINT / AUDIOBOOK

TITLE: _____

GENRE: _____

SERIES: _____

AUTHOR: _____

PAGES: _____

STARTED: _____

FINISHED: _____

☆ ☆ ☆ ☆ ☆

FORMAT READ: EBOOK / PRINT / AUDIOBOOK

✓ **SYNOPSIS/THINGS I LIKED:**

_____
_____
_____
_____
_____

🚫 **THINGS I DIDN'T LIKE:**

_____
_____
_____
_____
_____

✎ **FAVORITE QUOTE(S):**

_____
_____
_____
_____
_____
_____
_____
_____

TITLE: _____

GENRE: _____

SERIES: _____

AUTHOR: _____

PAGES: _____

STARTED: _____

FINISHED: _____

☆ ☆ ☆ ☆ ☆

FORMAT READ: EBOOK / PRINT / AUDIOBOOK

☑ **SYNOPSIS/THINGS I LIKED:**

_____
_____
_____
_____

🚫 **THINGS I DIDN'T LIKE:**

_____
_____
_____
_____

✎ **FAVORITE QUOTE(S):**

_____
_____
_____
_____
_____
_____

☑ **Synopsis/Things I liked:**

_____

_____

_____

_____

🚫 **Things I didn't like:**

_____

_____

_____

_____

✎ **Favorite quote(s):**

_____

_____

_____

_____

_____

_____

Title: _____

Genre: _____

Series: _____

Author: _____

Pages: _____

Started: _____

Finished: _____

☆☆☆☆☆

Format read: Ebook / Print / Audiobook

✔ SYNOPSIS/THINGS I LIKED:

_____

_____

_____

_____

🚫 THINGS I DIDN'T LIKE:

_____

_____

_____

_____

🖊 FAVORITE QUOTE(S):

_____

_____

_____

_____

_____

_____

TITLE: _____

GENRE: _____

SERIES: _____

AUTHOR: _____

PAGES: _____

STARTED: _____

FINISHED: _____

☆ ☆ ☆ ☆ ☆

FORMAT READ: EBOOK / PRINT / AUDIOBOOK

TITLE: _____

GENRE: _____

SERIES: _____

AUTHOR: _____

PAGES: _____

STARTED: _____

FINISHED: _____

☆ ☆ ☆ ☆ ☆

FORMAT READ: EBOOK / PRINT / AUDIOBOOK

✔ **SYNOPSIS/THINGS I LIKED:**

_____

_____

_____

_____

_____

🚫 **THINGS I DIDN'T LIKE:**

_____

_____

_____

_____

_____

✎ **FAVORITE QUOTE(S):**

_____

_____

_____

_____

_____

_____

_____

_____

TITLE: _____

GENRE: _____

SERIES: _____

AUTHOR: _____

PAGES: _____

STARTED: _____

FINISHED: _____

☆ ☆ ☆ ☆ ☆

FORMAT READ: EBOOK / PRINT / AUDIOBOOK

✓ **SYNOPSIS/THINGS I LIKED:**

_____
_____
_____
_____

🚫 **THINGS I DIDN'T LIKE:**

_____
_____
_____
_____

📝 **FAVORITE QUOTE(S):**

_____
_____
_____
_____
_____
_____
_____

✔ Synopsis/Things I liked:

_____
_____
_____
_____

🚫 Things I didn't like:

_____
_____
_____
_____

🖊 Favorite quote(s):

_____
_____
_____
_____
_____

Title: _____

Genre: _____

Series: _____

Author: _____

Pages: _____

Started: _____

Finished: _____

☆ ☆ ☆ ☆ ☆

Format read: Ebook / Print / Audiobook

✅ **SYNOPSIS/THINGS I LIKED:**

_____

_____

_____

_____

🚫 **THINGS I DIDN'T LIKE:**

_____

_____

_____

_____

📝 **FAVORITE QUOTE(S):**

_____

_____

_____

_____

_____

_____

TITLE: _____

GENRE: _____

SERIES: _____

AUTHOR: _____

PAGES: _____

STARTED: _____

FINISHED: _____

☆ ☆ ☆ ☆ ☆

FORMAT READ: EBOOK / PRINT / AUDIOBOOK

TITLE: _____

GENRE: _____

SERIES: _____

AUTHOR: _____

PAGES: _____

STARTED: _____

FINISHED: _____

☆ ☆ ☆ ☆ ☆

FORMAT READ: EBOOK / PRINT / AUDIOBOOK

✓ **SYNOPSIS/THINGS I LIKED:**

_____
_____
_____
_____
_____

🚫 **THINGS I DIDN'T LIKE:**

_____
_____
_____
_____
_____

✒ **FAVORITE QUOTE(S):**

_____
_____
_____
_____
_____
_____
_____
_____

TITLE: _____

GENRE: _____

SERIES: _____

AUTHOR: _____

PAGES: _____

STARTED: _____

FINISHED: _____

☆☆☆☆☆

FORMAT READ: EBOOK / PRINT / AUDIOBOOK

✔ **SYNOPSIS/THINGS I LIKED:**

_____
_____
_____
_____
_____

🚫 **THINGS I DIDN'T LIKE:**

_____
_____
_____
_____
_____

✏ **FAVORITE QUOTE(S):**

_____
_____
_____
_____
_____
_____
_____
_____

✔ **SYNOPSIS/THINGS I LIKED:**

_____
_____
_____
_____

🚫 **THINGS I DIDN'T LIKE:**

_____
_____
_____
_____

✎ **FAVORITE QUOTE(S):**

_____
_____
_____
_____
_____
_____

TITLE: _____

GENRE: _____

SERIES: _____

AUTHOR: _____

PAGES: _____

STARTED: _____

FINISHED: _____

☆ ☆ ☆ ☆ ☆

FORMAT READ: EBOOK / PRINT / AUDIOBOOK

✓ **SYNOPSIS/THINGS I LIKED:**

_____
_____
_____
_____

🚫 **THINGS I DIDN'T LIKE:**

_____
_____
_____
_____

✎ **FAVORITE QUOTE(S):**

_____
_____
_____
_____
_____
_____

TITLE: _____

GENRE: _____

SERIES: _____

AUTHOR: _____

PAGES: _____

STARTED: _____

FINISHED: _____

☆ ☆ ☆ ☆ ☆

FORMAT READ: EBOOK / PRINT / AUDIOBOOK

TITLE: _____

GENRE: _____

SERIES: _____

AUTHOR: _____

PAGES: _____

STARTED: _____

FINISHED: _____

☆ ☆ ☆ ☆ ☆

FORMAT READ: EBOOK / PRINT / AUDIOBOOK

☑ **SYNOPSIS/THINGS I LIKED:**

_____
_____
_____
_____

🚫 **THINGS I DIDN'T LIKE:**

_____
_____
_____
_____

✎ **FAVORITE QUOTE(S):**

_____
_____
_____
_____
_____
_____
_____

TITLE: _____

GENRE: _____

SERIES: _____

AUTHOR: _____

PAGES: _____

STARTED: _____

FINISHED: _____

☆☆☆☆☆

FORMAT READ: EBOOK / PRINT / AUDIOBOOK

✓ **SYNOPSIS/THINGS I LIKED:**

_____
_____
_____
_____

🚫 **THINGS I DIDN'T LIKE:**

_____
_____
_____
_____

✏️ **FAVORITE QUOTE(S):**

_____
_____
_____
_____
_____
_____
_____

✓ **SYNOPSIS/THINGS I LIKED:**

_____
_____
_____
_____

🚫 **THINGS I DIDN'T LIKE:**

_____
_____
_____
_____

📝 **FAVORITE QUOTE(S):**

_____
_____
_____
_____
_____
_____

TITLE: _____

GENRE: _____

SERIES: _____

AUTHOR: _____

PAGES: _____

STARTED: _____

FINISHED: _____

☆ ☆ ☆ ☆ ☆

FORMAT READ: EBOOK / PRINT / AUDIOBOOK

☑ **Synopsis/Things I liked:**

_____
_____
_____
_____

🚫 **Things I didn't like:**

_____
_____
_____
_____

✎ **Favorite quote(s):**

_____
_____
_____
_____
_____
_____

Title: _____

Genre: _____

Series: _____

Author: _____

Pages: _____

Started: _____

Finished: _____

☆ ☆ ☆ ☆ ☆

Format read: Ebook / Print / Audiobook

TITLE: _____

GENRE: _____

SERIES: _____

AUTHOR: _____

PAGES: _____

STARTED: _____

FINISHED: _____

☆☆☆☆☆

FORMAT READ: EBOOK / PRINT / AUDIOBOOK

✓ **SYNOPSIS/THINGS I LIKED:**

_____
_____
_____
_____

🚫 **THINGS I DIDN'T LIKE:**

_____
_____
_____
_____

✎ **FAVORITE QUOTE(S):**

_____
_____
_____
_____
_____
_____

TITLE: _____

GENRE: _____

SERIES: _____

AUTHOR: _____

PAGES: _____

STARTED: _____

FINISHED: _____

☆ ☆ ☆ ☆ ☆

FORMAT READ: EBOOK / PRINT / AUDIOBOOK

✓ **SYNOPSIS/THINGS I LIKED:**

_____
_____
_____
_____

🚫 **THINGS I DIDN'T LIKE:**

_____
_____
_____
_____

✐ **FAVORITE QUOTE(S):**

_____
_____
_____
_____
_____
_____

✓ **SYNOPSIS/THINGS I LIKED:**

_____

_____

_____

_____

🚫 **THINGS I DIDN'T LIKE:**

_____

_____

_____

_____

📝 **FAVORITE QUOTE(S):**

_____

_____

_____

_____

_____

_____

TITLE: _____

GENRE: _____

SERIES: _____

AUTHOR: _____

PAGES: _____

STARTED: _____

FINISHED: _____

☆ ☆ ☆ ☆ ☆

FORMAT READ: EBOOK / PRINT / AUDIOBOOK

✓ **SYNOPSIS/THINGS I LIKED:**

_____

_____

_____

_____

_____

🚫 **THINGS I DIDN'T LIKE:**

_____

_____

_____

_____

_____

✏️ **FAVORITE QUOTE(S):**

_____

_____

_____

_____

_____

_____

_____

_____

TITLE: _____

GENRE: _____

SERIES: _____

AUTHOR: _____

PAGES: _____

STARTED: _____

FINISHED: _____

☆ ☆ ☆ ☆ ☆

FORMAT READ: EBOOK / PRINT / AUDIOBOOK

TITLE: _____

GENRE: _____

SERIES: _____

AUTHOR: _____

PAGES: _____

STARTED: _____

FINISHED: _____

☆ ☆ ☆ ☆ ☆

FORMAT READ: EBOOK / PRINT / AUDIOBOOK

✔ SYNOPSIS/THINGS I LIKED:

_____
_____
_____
_____

🚫 THINGS I DIDN'T LIKE:

_____
_____
_____
_____

✎ FAVORITE QUOTE(S):

_____
_____
_____
_____
_____
_____
_____

TITLE: _____

GENRE: _____

SERIES: _____

AUTHOR: _____

PAGES: _____

STARTED: _____

FINISHED: _____

☆☆☆☆☆

FORMAT READ: EBOOK / PRINT / AUDIOBOOK

✓ **SYNOPSIS/THINGS I LIKED:**

_____
_____
_____
_____

🚫 **THINGS I DIDN'T LIKE:**

_____
_____
_____
_____

✏️ **FAVORITE QUOTE(S):**

_____
_____
_____
_____
_____
_____
_____

✓ **SYNOPSIS/THINGS I LIKED:**

_____
_____
_____
_____
_____
_____

🚫 **THINGS I DIDN'T LIKE:**

_____
_____
_____
_____
_____

✏️ **FAVORITE QUOTE(S):**

_____
_____
_____
_____
_____
_____
_____
_____

TITLE: _____

GENRE: _____

SERIES: _____

AUTHOR: _____

PAGES: _____

STARTED: _____

FINISHED: _____

☆ ☆ ☆ ☆ ☆

FORMAT READ: EBOOK / PRINT / AUDIOBOOK

✓ **SYNOPSIS/THINGS I LIKED:**

_____

_____

_____

_____

🚫 **THINGS I DIDN'T LIKE:**

_____

_____

_____

_____

✎ **FAVORITE QUOTE(S):**

_____

_____

_____

_____

_____

_____

TITLE: _____

GENRE: _____

SERIES: _____

AUTHOR: _____

PAGES: _____

STARTED: _____

FINISHED: _____

☆ ☆ ☆ ☆ ☆

FORMAT READ: EBOOK / PRINT / AUDIOBOOK

TITLE:

GENRE:

SERIES:

AUTHOR:

PAGES:

STARTED:

FINISHED:

☆ ☆ ☆ ☆ ☆

FORMAT READ: EBOOK / PRINT / AUDIOBOOK

✓ **SYNOPSIS/THINGS I LIKED:**

_____
_____
_____
_____

🚫 **THINGS I DIDN'T LIKE:**

_____
_____
_____
_____

✎ **FAVORITE QUOTE(S):**

_____
_____
_____
_____
_____
_____

TITLE: _____

GENRE: _____

SERIES: _____

AUTHOR: _____

PAGES: _____

STARTED: _____

FINISHED: _____

☆ ☆ ☆ ☆ ☆

FORMAT READ: EBOOK / PRINT / AUDIOBOOK

✓ **SYNOPSIS/THINGS I LIKED:**

_____
_____
_____
_____
_____

🚫 **THINGS I DIDN'T LIKE:**

_____
_____
_____
_____

✎ **FAVORITE QUOTE(S):**

_____
_____
_____
_____
_____
_____
_____

✓ **Synopsis/Things I liked:**

_____

_____

_____

_____

🚫 **Things I didn't like:**

_____

_____

_____

_____

✏️ **Favorite quote(s):**

_____

_____

_____

_____

_____

_____

Title: _____

Genre: _____

Series: _____

Author: _____

Pages: _____

Started: _____

Finished: _____

☆ ☆ ☆ ☆ ☆

Format read: Ebook / Print / Audiobook

✓ **SYNOPSIS/THINGS I LIKED:**

_____

_____

_____

_____

🚫 **THINGS I DIDN'T LIKE:**

_____

_____

_____

_____

✎ **FAVORITE QUOTE(S):**

_____

_____

_____

_____

_____

_____

TITLE: _____

GENRE: _____

SERIES: _____

AUTHOR: _____

PAGES: _____

STARTED: _____

FINISHED: _____

☆ ☆ ☆ ☆ ☆

FORMAT READ: EBOOK / PRINT / AUDIOBOOK

TITLE: _____

GENRE: _____

SERIES: _____

AUTHOR: _____

PAGES: _____

STARTED: _____

FINISHED: _____

☆ ☆ ☆ ☆ ☆

FORMAT READ: EBOOK / PRINT / AUDIOBOOK

✔ **SYNOPSIS/THINGS I LIKED:**

_____
_____
_____
_____
_____

🚫 **THINGS I DIDN'T LIKE:**

_____
_____
_____
_____
_____

📝 **FAVORITE QUOTE(S):**

_____
_____
_____
_____
_____
_____
_____
_____

TITLE: _____

GENRE: _____

SERIES: _____

AUTHOR: _____

PAGES: _____

STARTED: _____

FINISHED: _____

☆ ☆ ☆ ☆ ☆

FORMAT READ: EBOOK / PRINT / AUDIOBOOK

✔ **SYNOPSIS/THINGS I LIKED:**

_____
_____
_____
_____

🚫 **THINGS I DIDN'T LIKE:**

_____
_____
_____
_____

📝 **FAVORITE QUOTE(S):**

_____
_____
_____
_____
_____
_____
_____

☑ SYNOPSIS/THINGS I LIKED:

_____

_____

_____

_____

🚫 THINGS I DIDN'T LIKE:

_____

_____

_____

_____

✏ FAVORITE QUOTE(S):

_____

_____

_____

_____

_____

_____

TITLE: _____

GENRE: _____

SERIES: _____

AUTHOR: _____

PAGES: _____

STARTED: _____

FINISHED: _____

☆ ☆ ☆ ☆ ☆

FORMAT READ: EBOOK / PRINT / AUDIOBOOK

✓ SYNOPSIS/THINGS I LIKED:

_____
_____
_____
_____

🚫 THINGS I DIDN'T LIKE:

_____
_____
_____
_____
_____

✎ FAVORITE QUOTE(S):

_____
_____
_____
_____
_____
_____
_____

TITLE: _____

GENRE: _____

SERIES: _____

AUTHOR: _____

PAGES: _____

STARTED: _____

FINISHED: _____

☆ ☆ ☆ ☆ ☆

FORMAT READ: EBOOK / PRINT / AUDIOBOOK

TITLE: _____

GENRE: _____

SERIES: _____

AUTHOR: _____

PAGES: _____

STARTED: _____

FINISHED: _____

☆ ☆ ☆ ☆ ☆

FORMAT READ: EBOOK / PRINT / AUDIOBOOK

☑ SYNOPSIS/THINGS I LIKED:

_____
_____
_____
_____

🚫 THINGS I DIDN'T LIKE:

_____
_____
_____
_____

✏️ FAVORITE QUOTE(S):

_____
_____
_____
_____
_____
_____
_____

TITLE: _____

GENRE: _____

SERIES: _____

AUTHOR: _____

PAGES: _____

STARTED: _____

FINISHED: _____

☆☆☆☆☆

FORMAT READ: EBOOK / PRINT / AUDIOBOOK

☑ **SYNOPSIS/THINGS I LIKED:**

_____
_____
_____
_____

🚫 **THINGS I DIDN'T LIKE:**

_____
_____
_____
_____

🖊 **FAVORITE QUOTE(S):**

_____
_____
_____
_____
_____
_____
_____

✓ **SYNOPSIS/THINGS I LIKED:**

_____

_____

_____

_____

🚫 **THINGS I DIDN'T LIKE:**

_____

_____

_____

_____

✎ **FAVORITE QUOTE(S):**

_____

_____

_____

_____

_____

_____

_____

TITLE: _____

GENRE: _____

SERIES: _____

AUTHOR: _____

PAGES: _____

STARTED: _____

FINISHED: _____

☆ ☆ ☆ ☆ ☆

FORMAT READ: EBOOK / PRINT / AUDIOBOOK

✅ **Synopsis/Things I liked:**

_____

_____

_____

_____

_____

🚫 **Things I didn't like:**

_____

_____

_____

_____

✏️ **Favorite quote(s):**

_____

_____

_____

_____

_____

_____

_____

Title: _____

Genre: _____

Series: _____

Author: _____

Pages: _____

Started: _____

Finished: _____

☆ ☆ ☆ ☆ ☆

Format read: Ebook / Print / Audiobook

TITLE: _____

GENRE: _____

SERIES: _____

AUTHOR: _____

PAGES: _____

STARTED: _____

FINISHED: _____

☆ ☆ ☆ ☆ ☆

FORMAT READ: EBOOK / PRINT / AUDIOBOOK

✓ **SYNOPSIS/THINGS I LIKED:**

_____
_____
_____
_____
_____

🚫 **THINGS I DIDN'T LIKE:**

_____
_____
_____
_____

📝 **FAVORITE QUOTE(S):**

_____
_____
_____
_____
_____
_____
_____
_____

TITLE: _____

GENRE: _____

SERIES: _____

AUTHOR: _____

PAGES: _____

STARTED: _____

FINISHED: _____

☆☆☆☆☆

FORMAT READ: EBOOK / PRINT / AUDIOBOOK

✓ **SYNOPSIS/THINGS I LIKED:**

_____
_____
_____
_____
_____

🚫 **THINGS I DIDN'T LIKE:**

_____
_____
_____
_____
_____

✎ **FAVORITE QUOTE(S):**

_____
_____
_____
_____
_____
_____
_____
_____

✓ **SYNOPSIS/THINGS I LIKED:**

_____
_____
_____
_____

🚫 **THINGS I DIDN'T LIKE:**

_____
_____
_____
_____

✎ **FAVORITE QUOTE(S):**

_____
_____
_____
_____
_____
_____

TITLE: _____

GENRE: _____

SERIES: _____

AUTHOR: _____

PAGES: _____

STARTED: _____

FINISHED: _____

☆ ☆ ☆ ☆ ☆

FORMAT READ: EBOOK / PRINT / AUDIOBOOK

✅ **SYNOPSIS/THINGS I LIKED:**

_____

_____

_____

_____

🚫 **THINGS I DIDN'T LIKE:**

_____

_____

_____

_____

📝 **FAVORITE QUOTE(S):**

_____

_____

_____

_____

_____

_____

TITLE: _____

GENRE: _____

SERIES: _____

AUTHOR: _____

PAGES: _____

STARTED: _____

FINISHED: _____

☆ ☆ ☆ ☆ ☆

FORMAT READ: EBOOK / PRINT / AUDIOBOOK

188

TITLE: _____

GENRE: _____

SERIES: _____

AUTHOR: _____

PAGES: _____

STARTED: _____

FINISHED: _____

☆ ☆ ☆ ☆ ☆

FORMAT READ: EBOOK / PRINT / AUDIOBOOK

✔ **SYNOPSIS/THINGS I LIKED:**

_____
_____
_____
_____
_____

🚫 **THINGS I DIDN'T LIKE:**

_____
_____
_____
_____

📝 **FAVORITE QUOTE(S):**

_____
_____
_____
_____
_____
_____
_____
_____

TITLE: _____

GENRE: _____

SERIES: _____

AUTHOR: _____

PAGES: _____

STARTED: _____

FINISHED: _____

☆ ☆ ☆ ☆ ☆

FORMAT READ: EBOOK / PRINT / AUDIOBOOK

✓ **SYNOPSIS/THINGS I LIKED:**

_____
_____
_____
_____

🚫 **THINGS I DIDN'T LIKE:**

_____
_____
_____
_____

📝 **FAVORITE QUOTE(S):**

_____
_____
_____
_____
_____
_____
_____

☑ **SYNOPSIS/THINGS I LIKED:**

_____
_____
_____
_____

🚫 **THINGS I DIDN'T LIKE:**

_____
_____
_____
_____

📝 **FAVORITE QUOTE(S):**

_____
_____
_____
_____
_____
_____

TITLE: _____

GENRE: _____

SERIES: _____

AUTHOR: _____

PAGES: _____

STARTED: _____

FINISHED: _____

☆☆☆☆☆

FORMAT READ: EBOOK / PRINT / AUDIOBOOK

✅ **Synopsis/Things I liked:**

_____
_____
_____
_____
_____

🚫 **Things I didn't like:**

_____
_____
_____
_____
_____

✏️ **Favorite quote(s):**

_____
_____
_____
_____
_____
_____
_____

Title: _____

Genre: _____

Series: _____

Author: _____

Pages: _____

Started: _____

Finished: _____

☆ ☆ ☆ ☆ ☆

Format read: Ebook / Print / Audiobook

TITLE: _____

GENRE: _____

SERIES: _____

AUTHOR: _____

PAGES: _____

STARTED: _____

FINISHED: _____

☆ ☆ ☆ ☆ ☆

FORMAT READ: EBOOK / PRINT / AUDIOBOOK

✓ **SYNOPSIS/THINGS I LIKED:**

_____
_____
_____
_____
_____

🚫 **THINGS I DIDN'T LIKE:**

_____
_____
_____
_____
_____

✏️ **FAVORITE QUOTE(S):**

_____
_____
_____
_____
_____
_____
_____
_____

TITLE: _____

GENRE: _____

SERIES: _____

AUTHOR: _____

PAGES: _____

STARTED: _____

FINISHED: _____

☆ ☆ ☆ ☆ ☆

FORMAT READ: EBOOK / PRINT / AUDIOBOOK

✔ **SYNOPSIS/THINGS I LIKED:**

_____

_____

_____

_____

🚫 **THINGS I DIDN'T LIKE:**

_____

_____

_____

_____

✎ **FAVORITE QUOTE(S):**

_____

_____

_____

_____

_____

_____

_____

✓ **SYNOPSIS/THINGS I LIKED:**

_____

_____

_____

_____

_____

🚫 **THINGS I DIDN'T LIKE:**

_____

_____

_____

_____

✏️ **FAVORITE QUOTE(S):**

_____

_____

_____

_____

_____

_____

_____

TITLE: _____

GENRE: _____

SERIES: _____

AUTHOR: _____

PAGES: _____

STARTED: _____

FINISHED: _____

☆ ☆ ☆ ☆ ☆

FORMAT READ: EBOOK / PRINT / AUDIOBOOK

✓ **SYNOPSIS/THINGS I LIKED:**

_____

_____

_____

_____

_____

🚫 **THINGS I DIDN'T LIKE:**

_____

_____

_____

_____

✏️ **FAVORITE QUOTE(S):**

_____

_____

_____

_____

_____

_____

TITLE: _____

GENRE: _____

SERIES: _____

AUTHOR: _____

PAGES: _____

STARTED: _____

FINISHED: _____

☆ ☆ ☆ ☆ ☆

FORMAT READ: EBOOK / PRINT / AUDIOBOOK

196

TITLE: _____

GENRE: _____

SERIES: _____

AUTHOR: _____

PAGES: _____

STARTED: _____

FINISHED: _____

☆ ☆ ☆ ☆ ☆

FORMAT READ: EBOOK / PRINT / AUDIOBOOK

✓ **SYNOPSIS/THINGS I LIKED:**

_____
_____
_____
_____
_____

🚫 **THINGS I DIDN'T LIKE:**

_____
_____
_____
_____

✎ **FAVORITE QUOTE(S):**

_____
_____
_____
_____
_____
_____
_____

TITLE: _____

GENRE: _____

SERIES: _____

AUTHOR: _____

PAGES: _____

STARTED: _____

FINISHED: _____

☆☆☆☆☆

FORMAT READ: EBOOK / PRINT / AUDIOBOOK

✓ **SYNOPSIS/THINGS I LIKED:**

_____
_____
_____
_____

🚫 **THINGS I DIDN'T LIKE:**

_____
_____
_____
_____

📝 **FAVORITE QUOTE(S):**

_____
_____
_____
_____
_____
_____

✓ **SYNOPSIS/THINGS I LIKED:**

_____

_____

_____

_____

🚫 **THINGS I DIDN'T LIKE:**

_____

_____

_____

_____

✎ **FAVORITE QUOTE(S):**

_____

_____

_____

_____

_____

_____

_____

TITLE: _____

GENRE: _____

SERIES: _____

AUTHOR: _____

PAGES: _____

STARTED: _____

FINISHED: _____

☆ ☆ ☆ ☆ ☆

FORMAT READ: EBOOK / PRINT / AUDIOBOOK

✔ **SYNOPSIS/THINGS I LIKED:**

_____
_____
_____
_____

🚫 **THINGS I DIDN'T LIKE:**

_____
_____
_____
_____

✎ **FAVORITE QUOTE(S):**

_____
_____
_____
_____
_____
_____

TITLE: _____

GENRE: _____

SERIES: _____

AUTHOR: _____

PAGES: _____

STARTED: _____

FINISHED: _____

☆ ☆ ☆ ☆ ☆

FORMAT READ: EBOOK / PRINT / AUDIOBOOK

TITLE: _____

GENRE: _____

SERIES: _____

AUTHOR: _____

PAGES: _____

STARTED: _____

FINISHED: _____

☆ ☆ ☆ ☆ ☆

FORMAT READ: EBOOK / PRINT / AUDIOBOOK

✓ **SYNOPSIS/THINGS I LIKED:**

_____
_____
_____
_____

🚫 **THINGS I DIDN'T LIKE:**

_____
_____
_____
_____

✏️ **FAVORITE QUOTE(S):**

_____
_____
_____
_____
_____
_____

TITLE: _____

GENRE: _____

SERIES: _____

AUTHOR: _____

PAGES: _____

STARTED: _____

FINISHED: _____

☆☆☆☆☆

FORMAT READ: EBOOK / PRINT / AUDIOBOOK

✓ SYNOPSIS/THINGS I LIKED:

_____
_____
_____
_____

🚫 THINGS I DIDN'T LIKE:

_____
_____
_____
_____

✎ FAVORITE QUOTE(S):

_____
_____
_____
_____
_____
_____
_____

✓ **SYNOPSIS/THINGS I LIKED:**

_____
_____
_____
_____

🚫 **THINGS I DIDN'T LIKE:**

_____
_____
_____
_____

✎ **FAVORITE QUOTE(S):**

_____
_____
_____
_____
_____
_____
_____

TITLE: _____

GENRE: _____

SERIES: _____

AUTHOR: _____

PAGES: _____

STARTED: _____

FINISHED: _____

☆ ☆ ☆ ☆ ☆

FORMAT READ: EBOOK / PRINT / AUDIOBOOK

✅ **SYNOPSIS/THINGS I LIKED:**

_____

_____

_____

_____

🚫 **THINGS I DIDN'T LIKE:**

_____

_____

_____

_____

📝 **FAVORITE QUOTE(S):**

_____

_____

_____

_____

_____

_____

TITLE: _____

GENRE: _____

SERIES: _____

AUTHOR: _____

PAGES: _____

STARTED: _____

FINISHED: _____

☆ ☆ ☆ ☆ ☆

FORMAT READ: EBOOK / PRINT / AUDIOBOOK

TITLE: _____

GENRE: _____

SERIES: _____

AUTHOR: _____

PAGES: _____

STARTED: _____

FINISHED: _____

☆ ☆ ☆ ☆ ☆

FORMAT READ: EBOOK / PRINT / AUDIOBOOK

✓ **SYNOPSIS/THINGS I LIKED:**

_____
_____
_____
_____
_____

🚫 **THINGS I DIDN'T LIKE:**

_____
_____
_____
_____
_____

✏️ **FAVORITE QUOTE(S):**

_____
_____
_____
_____
_____
_____
_____

TITLE: _____

GENRE: _____

SERIES: _____

AUTHOR: _____

PAGES: _____

STARTED: _____

FINISHED: _____

☆ ☆ ☆ ☆ ☆

FORMAT READ: EBOOK / PRINT / AUDIOBOOK

✓ **SYNOPSIS/THINGS I LIKED:**

_____
_____
_____
_____

🚫 **THINGS I DIDN'T LIKE:**

_____
_____
_____
_____

✎ **FAVORITE QUOTE(S):**

_____
_____
_____
_____
_____
_____
_____

✓ SYNOPSIS/THINGS I LIKED:

_____

_____

_____

_____

🚫 THINGS I DIDN'T LIKE:

_____

_____

_____

_____

✎ FAVORITE QUOTE(S):

_____

_____

_____

_____

_____

_____

TITLE: _____

GENRE: _____

SERIES: _____

AUTHOR: _____

PAGES: _____

STARTED: _____

FINISHED: _____

☆ ☆ ☆ ☆ ☆

FORMAT READ: EBOOK / PRINT / AUDIOBOOK

✓ **SYNOPSIS/THINGS I LIKED:**

_____

_____

_____

_____

⊘ **THINGS I DIDN'T LIKE:**

_____

_____

_____

_____

✎ **FAVORITE QUOTE(S):**

_____

_____

_____

_____

_____

_____

TITLE: _____

GENRE: _____

SERIES: _____

AUTHOR: _____

PAGES: _____

STARTED: _____

FINISHED: _____

☆ ☆ ☆ ☆ ☆

FORMAT READ: EBOOK / PRINT / AUDIOBOOK

TITLE: _____

GENRE: _____

SERIES: _____

AUTHOR: _____

PAGES: _____

STARTED: _____

FINISHED: _____

☆ ☆ ☆ ☆ ☆

FORMAT READ: EBOOK / PRINT / AUDIOBOOK

✓ SYNOPSIS/THINGS I LIKED:

_____
_____
_____
_____
_____

🚫 THINGS I DIDN'T LIKE:

_____
_____
_____
_____
_____

✎ FAVORITE QUOTE(S):

_____
_____
_____
_____
_____
_____
_____
_____

TITLE: _____

GENRE: _____

SERIES: _____

AUTHOR: _____

PAGES: _____

STARTED: _____

FINISHED: _____

☆☆☆☆☆

FORMAT READ: EBOOK / PRINT / AUDIOBOOK

✓ SYNOPSIS/THINGS I LIKED:
_____
_____
_____
_____
_____

⊘ THINGS I DIDN'T LIKE:
_____
_____
_____
_____

✎ FAVORITE QUOTE(S):
_____
_____
_____
_____
_____
_____
_____

☑ **Synopsis/Things I liked:**

_____
_____
_____
_____

🚫 **Things I didn't like:**

_____
_____
_____
_____
_____

✎ **Favorite quote(s):**

_____
_____
_____
_____
_____
_____

Title: _____

Genre: _____

Series: _____

Author: _____

Pages: _____

Started: _____

Finished: _____

☆ ☆ ☆ ☆ ☆

Format read: Ebook / Print / Audiobook

✅ **SYNOPSIS/THINGS I LIKED:**

_____

_____

_____

_____

🚫 **THINGS I DIDN'T LIKE:**

_____

_____

_____

_____

✏️ **FAVORITE QUOTE(S):**

_____

_____

_____

_____

_____

_____

TITLE: _____

GENRE: _____

SERIES: _____

AUTHOR: _____

PAGES: _____

STARTED: _____

FINISHED: _____

☆ ☆ ☆ ☆ ☆

FORMAT READ: EBOOK / PRINT / AUDIOBOOK

TITLE: _____

GENRE: _____

SERIES: _____

AUTHOR: _____

PAGES: _____

STARTED: _____

FINISHED: _____

☆ ☆ ☆ ☆ ☆

FORMAT READ: EBOOK / PRINT / AUDIOBOOK

✓ SYNOPSIS/THINGS I LIKED:

_____
_____
_____
_____
_____

🚫 THINGS I DIDN'T LIKE:

_____
_____
_____
_____
_____

✎ FAVORITE QUOTE(S):

_____
_____
_____
_____
_____
_____
_____
_____
_____

TITLE: _____

GENRE: _____

SERIES: _____

AUTHOR: _____

PAGES: _____

STARTED: _____

FINISHED: _____

☆☆☆☆☆

FORMAT READ: EBOOK / PRINT / AUDIOBOOK

✓ **SYNOPSIS/THINGS I LIKED:**

_____
_____
_____
_____

🚫 **THINGS I DIDN'T LIKE:**

_____
_____
_____
_____

✏️ **FAVORITE QUOTE(S):**

_____
_____
_____
_____
_____
_____
_____
_____

✓ **SYNOPSIS/THINGS I LIKED:**

_____

_____

_____

_____

_____

🚫 **THINGS I DIDN'T LIKE:**

_____

_____

_____

_____

✎ **FAVORITE QUOTE(S):**

_____

_____

_____

_____

_____

_____

TITLE: _____

GENRE: _____

SERIES: _____

AUTHOR: _____

PAGES: _____

STARTED: _____

FINISHED: _____

☆ ☆ ☆ ☆ ☆

FORMAT READ: EBOOK / PRINT / AUDIOBOOK

✅ **SYNOPSIS/THINGS I LIKED:**

_____

_____

_____

_____

🚫 **THINGS I DIDN'T LIKE:**

_____

_____

_____

_____

✏️ **FAVORITE QUOTE(S):**

_____

_____

_____

_____

_____

_____

TITLE: _____

GENRE: _____

SERIES: _____

AUTHOR: _____

PAGES: _____

STARTED: _____

FINISHED: _____

☆☆☆☆☆

FORMAT READ: EBOOK / PRINT / AUDIOBOOK

TITLE: _____

GENRE: _____

SERIES: _____

AUTHOR: _____

PAGES: _____

STARTED: _____

FINISHED: _____

☆ ☆ ☆ ☆ ☆

FORMAT READ: EBOOK / PRINT / AUDIOBOOK

☑ **SYNOPSIS/THINGS I LIKED:**

_____
_____
_____
_____
_____

🚫 **THINGS I DIDN'T LIKE:**

_____
_____
_____
_____

✏️ **FAVORITE QUOTE(S):**

_____
_____
_____
_____
_____
_____
_____
_____

TITLE: _____

GENRE: _____

SERIES: _____

AUTHOR: _____

PAGES: _____

STARTED: _____

FINISHED: _____

☆☆☆☆☆

FORMAT READ: EBOOK / PRINT / AUDIOBOOK

✓ **SYNOPSIS/THINGS I LIKED:**

_____
_____
_____
_____

🚫 **THINGS I DIDN'T LIKE:**

_____
_____
_____
_____

✏️ **FAVORITE QUOTE(S):**

_____
_____
_____
_____
_____
_____
_____

✔ **SYNOPSIS/THINGS I LIKED:**

_____

_____

_____

_____

🚫 **THINGS I DIDN'T LIKE:**

_____

_____

_____

_____

✎ **FAVORITE QUOTE(S):**

_____

_____

_____

_____

_____

TITLE: _____

GENRE: _____

SERIES: _____

AUTHOR: _____

PAGES: _____

STARTED: _____

FINISHED: _____

☆ ☆ ☆ ☆ ☆

FORMAT READ: EBOOK / PRINT / AUDIOBOOK

✓ **Synopsis/Things I liked:**

_____
_____
_____
_____
_____

🚫 **Things I didn't like:**

_____
_____
_____
_____
_____

✎ **Favorite quote(s):**

_____
_____
_____
_____
_____
_____
_____

Title: _____

Genre: _____

Series: _____

Author: _____

Pages: _____

Started: _____

Finished: _____

☆ ☆ ☆ ☆ ☆

Format read: Ebook / Print / Audiobook

TITLE: _____

GENRE: _____

SERIES: _____

AUTHOR: _____

PAGES: _____

STARTED: _____

FINISHED: _____

☆ ☆ ☆ ☆ ☆

FORMAT READ: EBOOK / PRINT / AUDIOBOOK

✓ SYNOPSIS/THINGS I LIKED:

_____
_____
_____
_____
_____

🚫 THINGS I DIDN'T LIKE:

_____
_____
_____
_____
_____

✎ FAVORITE QUOTE(S):

_____
_____
_____
_____
_____
_____
_____
_____

TITLE: _____

GENRE: _____

SERIES: _____

AUTHOR: _____

PAGES: _____

STARTED: _____

FINISHED: _____

☆☆☆☆☆

FORMAT READ: EBOOK / PRINT / AUDIOBOOK

✓ **SYNOPSIS/THINGS I LIKED:**

_____
_____
_____
_____
_____

🚫 **THINGS I DIDN'T LIKE:**

_____
_____
_____
_____
_____

✏️ **FAVORITE QUOTE(S):**

_____
_____
_____
_____
_____
_____
_____
_____

✔ Synopsis/Things I liked:

_____
_____
_____
_____
_____

🚫 Things I didn't like:

_____
_____
_____
_____

✎ Favorite quote(s):

_____
_____
_____
_____
_____
_____

Title: _____

Genre: _____

Series: _____

Author: _____

Pages: _____

Started: _____

Finished: _____

☆ ☆ ☆ ☆ ☆

Format read: Ebook / Print / Audiobook

✓ **SYNOPSIS/THINGS I LIKED:**

_____

_____

_____

_____

_____

🚫 **THINGS I DIDN'T LIKE:**

_____

_____

_____

_____

✎ **FAVORITE QUOTE(S):**

_____

_____

_____

_____

_____

_____

_____

TITLE: _____

GENRE: _____

SERIES: _____

AUTHOR: _____

PAGES: _____

STARTED: _____

FINISHED: _____

☆ ☆ ☆ ☆ ☆

FORMAT READ: EBOOK / PRINT / AUDIOBOOK

TITLE: _____

GENRE: _____

SERIES: _____

AUTHOR: _____

PAGES: _____

STARTED: _____

FINISHED: _____

☆ ☆ ☆ ☆ ☆

FORMAT READ: EBOOK / PRINT / AUDIOBOOK

✓ SYNOPSIS/THINGS I LIKED:
_____
_____
_____
_____
_____

🚫 THINGS I DIDN'T LIKE:
_____
_____
_____
_____

✏️ FAVORITE QUOTE(S):
_____
_____
_____
_____
_____
_____
_____
_____

TITLE: _____

GENRE: _____

SERIES: _____

AUTHOR: _____

PAGES: _____

STARTED: _____

FINISHED: _____

☆ ☆ ☆ ☆ ☆

FORMAT READ: EBOOK / PRINT / AUDIOBOOK

✓ **SYNOPSIS/THINGS I LIKED:**

_____
_____
_____
_____
_____

🚫 **THINGS I DIDN'T LIKE:**

_____
_____
_____
_____
_____

✎ **FAVORITE QUOTE(S):**

_____
_____
_____
_____
_____
_____
_____
_____

226

✓ **SYNOPSIS/THINGS I LIKED:**

_____

_____

_____

_____

_____

🚫 **THINGS I DIDN'T LIKE:**

_____

_____

_____

_____

✎ **FAVORITE QUOTE(S):**

_____

_____

_____

_____

_____

_____

_____

TITLE: _____

GENRE: _____

SERIES: _____

AUTHOR: _____

PAGES: _____

STARTED: _____

FINISHED: _____

☆ ☆ ☆ ☆ ☆

FORMAT READ: EBOOK / PRINT / AUDIOBOOK

☑ **Synopsis/Things I liked:**

_____
_____
_____
_____
_____

🚫 **Things I didn't like:**

_____
_____
_____
_____
_____

✎ **Favorite quote(s):**

_____
_____
_____
_____
_____
_____
_____

Title: _____

Genre: _____

Series: _____

Author: _____

Pages: _____

Started: _____

Finished: _____

☆ ☆ ☆ ☆ ☆

Format read: Ebook / Print / Audiobook

TITLE: _____

GENRE: _____

SERIES: _____

AUTHOR: _____

PAGES: _____

STARTED: _____

FINISHED: _____

☆ ☆ ☆ ☆ ☆

FORMAT READ: EBOOK / PRINT / AUDIOBOOK

✓ SYNOPSIS/THINGS I LIKED:

_____
_____
_____
_____
_____

🚫 THINGS I DIDN'T LIKE:

_____
_____
_____
_____

✏️ FAVORITE QUOTE(S):

_____
_____
_____
_____
_____
_____
_____
_____

TITLE: _____

GENRE: _____

SERIES: _____

AUTHOR: _____

PAGES: _____

STARTED: _____

FINISHED: _____

☆☆☆☆☆

FORMAT READ: EBOOK / PRINT / AUDIOBOOK

✔ **SYNOPSIS/THINGS I LIKED:**

_____

_____

_____

_____

🚫 **THINGS I DIDN'T LIKE:**

_____

_____

_____

_____

✎ **FAVORITE QUOTE(S):**

_____

_____

_____

_____

_____

_____

_____

✔ **SYNOPSIS/THINGS I LIKED:**

_____

_____

_____

_____

_____

🚫 **THINGS I DIDN'T LIKE:**

_____

_____

_____

_____

✎ **FAVORITE QUOTE(S):**

_____

_____

_____

_____

_____

_____

TITLE: _____

GENRE: _____

SERIES: _____

AUTHOR: _____

PAGES: _____

STARTED: _____

FINISHED: _____

☆ ☆ ☆ ☆ ☆

FORMAT READ: EBOOK / PRINT / AUDIOBOOK

✓ **SYNOPSIS/THINGS I LIKED:**

_____

_____

_____

_____

_____

🚫 **THINGS I DIDN'T LIKE:**

_____

_____

_____

_____

_____

✎ **FAVORITE QUOTE(S):**

_____

_____

_____

_____

_____

_____

_____

_____

TITLE: _____

GENRE: _____

SERIES: _____

AUTHOR: _____

PAGES: _____

STARTED: _____

FINISHED: _____

☆ ☆ ☆ ☆ ☆

FORMAT READ: EBOOK / PRINT / AUDIOBOOK

TITLE:

GENRE:

SERIES:

AUTHOR:

PAGES:

STARTED:

FINISHED:

☆ ☆ ☆ ☆ ☆

FORMAT READ: EBOOK / PRINT / AUDIOBOOK

✔ SYNOPSIS/THINGS I LIKED:

🚫 THINGS I DIDN'T LIKE:

✎ FAVORITE QUOTE(S):

TITLE: _____

GENRE: _____

SERIES: _____

AUTHOR: _____

PAGES: _____

STARTED: _____

FINISHED: _____

☆☆☆☆☆

FORMAT READ: EBOOK / PRINT / AUDIOBOOK

✓ **SYNOPSIS/THINGS I LIKED:**

_____
_____
_____
_____
_____

🚫 **THINGS I DIDN'T LIKE:**

_____
_____
_____
_____

✏️ **FAVORITE QUOTE(S):**

_____
_____
_____
_____
_____
_____
_____

✔️ **Synopsis/Things I liked:**

_____
_____
_____
_____

🚫 **Things I didn't like:**

_____
_____
_____
_____

✏️ **Favorite quote(s):**

_____
_____
_____
_____
_____
_____
_____

Title: _____

Genre: _____

Series: _____

Author: _____

Pages: _____

Started: _____

Finished: _____

☆☆☆☆☆

Format read: Ebook / Print / Audiobook

✓ **Synopsis/Things I liked:**

_____

_____

_____

_____

🚫 **Things I didn't like:**

_____

_____

_____

_____

✎ **Favorite quote(s):**

_____

_____

_____

_____

_____

_____

_____

_____

TITLE: _____

GENRE: _____

SERIES: _____

AUTHOR: _____

PAGES: _____

STARTED: _____

FINISHED: _____

☆ ☆ ☆ ☆ ☆

FORMAT READ: EBOOK / PRINT / AUDIOBOOK

TITLE: _____

GENRE: _____

SERIES: _____

AUTHOR: _____

PAGES: _____

STARTED: _____

FINISHED: _____

☆ ☆ ☆ ☆ ☆

FORMAT READ: EBOOK / PRINT / AUDIOBOOK

✓ **SYNOPSIS/THINGS I LIKED:**

_____
_____
_____
_____

🚫 **THINGS I DIDN'T LIKE:**

_____
_____
_____
_____

📝 **FAVORITE QUOTE(S):**

_____
_____
_____
_____
_____
_____

TITLE: _____

GENRE: _____

SERIES: _____

AUTHOR: _____

PAGES: _____

STARTED: _____

FINISHED: _____

☆ ☆ ☆ ☆ ☆

FORMAT READ: EBOOK / PRINT / AUDIOBOOK

✓ **SYNOPSIS/THINGS I LIKED:**

_____
_____
_____
_____

🚫 **THINGS I DIDN'T LIKE:**

_____
_____
_____
_____

✏️ **FAVORITE QUOTE(S):**

_____
_____
_____
_____
_____
_____

✓ SYNOPSIS/THINGS I LIKED:
_____
_____
_____
_____
_____

🚫 THINGS I DIDN'T LIKE:
_____
_____
_____
_____

✏️ FAVORITE QUOTE(S):
_____
_____
_____
_____
_____
_____
_____

TITLE: _____

GENRE: _____

SERIES: _____

AUTHOR: _____

PAGES: _____

STARTED: _____

FINISHED: _____

☆ ☆ ☆ ☆ ☆

FORMAT READ: EBOOK / PRINT / AUDIOBOOK

✅ **SYNOPSIS/THINGS I LIKED:**

_____

_____

_____

_____

🚫 **THINGS I DIDN'T LIKE:**

_____

_____

_____

_____

📝 **FAVORITE QUOTE(S):**

_____

_____

_____

_____

_____

_____

TITLE: _____

GENRE: _____

SERIES: _____

AUTHOR: _____

PAGES: _____

STARTED: _____

FINISHED: _____

☆ ☆ ☆ ☆ ☆

FORMAT READ: EBOOK / PRINT / AUDIOBOOK

TITLE: _____

GENRE: _____

SERIES: _____

AUTHOR: _____

PAGES: _____

STARTED: _____

FINISHED: _____

☆☆☆☆☆

FORMAT READ: EBOOK / PRINT / AUDIOBOOK

✓ **SYNOPSIS/THINGS I LIKED:**

_____
_____
_____
_____

🚫 **THINGS I DIDN'T LIKE:**

_____
_____
_____
_____

✎ **FAVORITE QUOTE(S):**

_____
_____
_____
_____
_____
_____
_____

TITLE: _____

GENRE: _____

SERIES: _____

AUTHOR: _____

PAGES: _____

STARTED: _____

FINISHED: _____

☆☆☆☆☆

FORMAT READ: EBOOK / PRINT / AUDIOBOOK

✅ **SYNOPSIS/THINGS I LIKED:**

_____

_____

_____

_____

🚫 **THINGS I DIDN'T LIKE:**

_____

_____

_____

_____

📝 **FAVORITE QUOTE(S):**

_____

_____

_____

_____

_____

_____

☑ **Synopsis/Things I liked:**

_____
_____
_____
_____
_____

🚫 **Things I didn't like:**

_____
_____
_____
_____

✎ **Favorite quote(s):**

_____
_____
_____
_____
_____
_____
_____

Title: _____

Genre: _____

Series: _____

Author: _____

Pages: _____

Started: _____

Finished: _____

☆ ☆ ☆ ☆ ☆

Format read: Ebook / Print / Audiobook

☑ **Synopsis/Things I liked:**

_____
_____
_____
_____
_____

🚫 **Things I didn't like:**

_____
_____
_____
_____

✎ **Favorite quote(s):**

_____
_____
_____
_____
_____
_____
_____

Title: _____

Genre: _____

Series: _____

Author: _____

Pages: _____

Started: _____

Finished: _____

☆ ☆ ☆ ☆ ☆

Format read: Ebook / Print / Audiobook

TITLE: _____

GENRE: _____

SERIES: _____

AUTHOR: _____

PAGES: _____

STARTED: _____

FINISHED: _____

☆ ☆ ☆ ☆ ☆

FORMAT READ: EBOOK / PRINT / AUDIOBOOK

✓ **SYNOPSIS/THINGS I LIKED:**

_____
_____
_____
_____
_____

🚫 **THINGS I DIDN'T LIKE:**

_____
_____
_____
_____
_____

✎ **FAVORITE QUOTE(S):**

_____
_____
_____
_____
_____
_____
_____

TITLE: _____

GENRE: _____

SERIES: _____

AUTHOR: _____

PAGES: _____

STARTED: _____

FINISHED: _____

☆ ☆ ☆ ☆ ☆

FORMAT READ: EBOOK / PRINT / AUDIOBOOK

✓ **SYNOPSIS/THINGS I LIKED:**

_____
_____
_____
_____
_____

🚫 **THINGS I DIDN'T LIKE:**

_____
_____
_____
_____
_____

✎ **FAVORITE QUOTE(S):**

_____
_____
_____
_____
_____
_____
_____
_____

✔ **Synopsis/Things I liked:**

_____
_____
_____
_____
_____

🚫 **Things I didn't like:**

_____
_____
_____
_____

✎ **Favorite quote(s):**

_____
_____
_____
_____
_____
_____
_____

Title: _____

Genre: _____

Series: _____

Author: _____

Pages: _____

Started: _____

Finished: _____

☆ ☆ ☆ ☆ ☆

Format read: Ebook / Print / Audiobook

247

✓ **Synopsis/Things I liked:**

_____

_____

_____

_____

🚫 **Things I didn't like:**

_____

_____

_____

_____

✏️ **Favorite quote(s):**

_____

_____

_____

_____

_____

_____

Title: _____

Genre: _____

Series: _____

Author: _____

Pages: _____

Started: _____

Finished: _____

☆ ☆ ☆ ☆ ☆

Format read: Ebook / Print / Audiobook

TITLE: _____

GENRE: _____

SERIES: _____

AUTHOR: _____

PAGES: _____

STARTED: _____

FINISHED: _____

☆ ☆ ☆ ☆ ☆

FORMAT READ: EBOOK / PRINT / AUDIOBOOK

✔ **SYNOPSIS/THINGS I LIKED:**

_____
_____
_____
_____

🚫 **THINGS I DIDN'T LIKE:**

_____
_____
_____
_____

✎ **FAVORITE QUOTE(S):**

_____
_____
_____
_____
_____
_____
_____

TITLE: _____

GENRE: _____

SERIES: _____

AUTHOR: _____

PAGES: _____

STARTED: _____

FINISHED: _____

☆ ☆ ☆ ☆ ☆

FORMAT READ: EBOOK / PRINT / AUDIOBOOK

✓ **SYNOPSIS/THINGS I LIKED:**

_____
_____
_____
_____
_____

🚫 **THINGS I DIDN'T LIKE:**

_____
_____
_____
_____

✎ **FAVORITE QUOTE(S):**

_____
_____
_____
_____
_____
_____
_____

THE DUSTY
DNFs
(DID NOT FINISH)

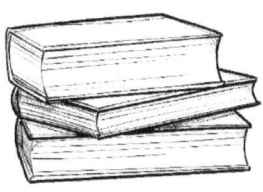

TITLE/PROGRESS:

COMMENTARY:

TITLE/PROGRESS:

COMMENTARY:

TITLE/PROGRESS:

COMMENTARY:

TITLE/PROGRESS:

COMMENTARY:

TITLE/PROGRESS:

COMMENTARY:

TITLE/PROGRESS:

COMMENTARY:

TITLE/PROGRESS:

COMMENTARY:

TITLE/PROGRESS:

COMMENTARY:

TITLE/PROGRESS:

COMMENTARY:

TITLE/PROGRESS:

COMMENTARY:

TITLE/PROGRESS:

COMMENTARY:

TITLE/PROGRESS:

COMMENTARY:

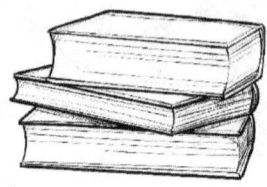

THE DUSTY
DNFs
(DID NOT FINISH)

TITLE/PROGRESS:

COMMENTARY:

TITLE/PROGRESS:

COMMENTARY:

TITLE/PROGRESS:

COMMENTARY:

TITLE/PROGRESS:

COMMENTARY:

TITLE/PROGRESS:

COMMENTARY:

TITLE/PROGRESS:

COMMENTARY:

TITLE/PROGRESS:

COMMENTARY:

TITLE/PROGRESS:

COMMENTARY:

TITLE/PROGRESS:

COMMENTARY:

TITLE/PROGRESS:

COMMENTARY:

TITLE/PROGRESS:

COMMENTARY:

TITLE/PROGRESS:

COMMENTARY:

THE DUSTY
DNFs
(DID NOT FINISH)

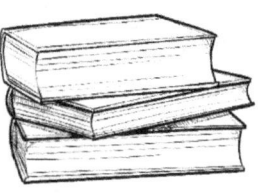

TITLE/PROGRESS:
_____

COMMENTARY:
_____

TITLE/PROGRESS:
_____

COMMENTARY:
_____

TITLE/PROGRESS:
_____

COMMENTARY:
_____

TITLE/PROGRESS:
_____

COMMENTARY:
_____

TITLE/PROGRESS:
_____

COMMENTARY:
_____

TITLE/PROGRESS:
_____

COMMENTARY:
_____

TITLE/PROGRESS:
_____

COMMENTARY:
_____

TITLE/PROGRESS:
_____

COMMENTARY:
_____

TITLE/PROGRESS:
_____

COMMENTARY:
_____

TITLE/PROGRESS:
_____

COMMENTARY:
_____

TITLE/PROGRESS:
_____

COMMENTARY:
_____

TITLE/PROGRESS:
_____

COMMENTARY:

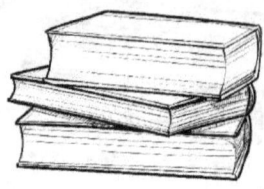

THE DUSTY
DNFs
(DID NOT FINISH)

TITLE/PROGRESS:
_____

COMMENTARY:
_____

TITLE/PROGRESS:
_____

COMMENTARY:
_____

TITLE/PROGRESS:
_____

COMMENTARY:
_____

TITLE/PROGRESS:
_____

COMMENTARY:
_____

TITLE/PROGRESS:
_____

COMMENTARY:
_____

TITLE/PROGRESS:
_____

COMMENTARY:
_____

TITLE/PROGRESS:
_____

COMMENTARY:
_____

TITLE/PROGRESS:
_____

COMMENTARY:
_____

TITLE/PROGRESS:
_____

COMMENTARY:
_____

TITLE/PROGRESS:
_____

COMMENTARY:
_____

TITLE/PROGRESS:
_____

COMMENTARY:
_____

THE DUSTY
DNFS
(DID NOT FINISH)

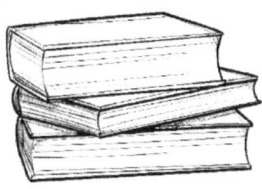

TITLE/PROGRESS:
_____

COMMENTARY:
_____

TITLE/PROGRESS:
_____

COMMENTARY:
_____

TITLE/PROGRESS:
_____

COMMENTARY:
_____

TITLE/PROGRESS:
_____

COMMENTARY:
_____

TITLE/PROGRESS:
_____

COMMENTARY:
_____

TITLE/PROGRESS:
_____

COMMENTARY:
_____

TITLE/PROGRESS:
_____

COMMENTARY:
_____

TITLE/PROGRESS:
_____

COMMENTARY:
_____

TITLE/PROGRESS:
_____

COMMENTARY:
_____

TITLE/PROGRESS:
_____

COMMENTARY:
_____

TITLE/PROGRESS:
_____

COMMENTARY:
_____

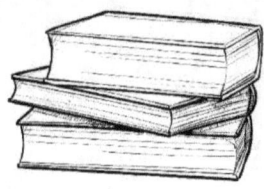

THE DUSTY
DNFS
(DID NOT FINISH)

TITLE/PROGRESS:

COMMENTARY:

TITLE/PROGRESS:

COMMENTARY:

TITLE/PROGRESS:

COMMENTARY:

TITLE/PROGRESS:

COMMENTARY:

TITLE/PROGRESS:

COMMENTARY:

TITLE/PROGRESS:

COMMENTARY:

TITLE/PROGRESS:

COMMENTARY:

TITLE/PROGRESS:

COMMENTARY:

TITLE/PROGRESS:

COMMENTARY:

TITLE/PROGRESS:

COMMENTARY:

TITLE/PROGRESS:

COMMENTARY:

Grab your replacement book journal!

Pick up your next volume now!

Paper and Ink Trophies and *Titles & Treasures* are both premium book journals also offered by Painted Wings Publishing. They each accommodate entries for 250 books and have individual aesthetic touches.

For more information, go to JHouserWrites.com

Free short story & more for newsletter subscribers!

Book Recommendations

THE
SEEDER WARS TRILOGY

THE
HEIR'S DUOLOGY

Seeder Wars is a Young Adult Contemporary Romantic Fantasy series featuring unique magic, botanical beings, spies, & assassins. The series starts with a central trilogy and expands to a spin-off duology (& more on the way!)

Magic in the Match is a series of standalone Adult Fairy Tale Sweet Romances.

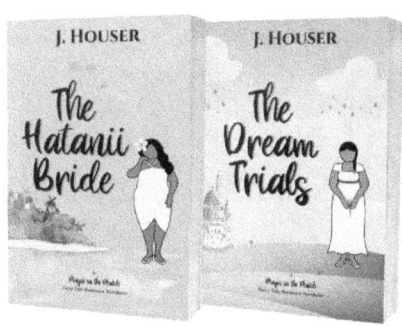

Magic in the Match
Fairy Tale
Romances

The Hatanii Bride is a novelette inspired by a Polish fairy tale (*The Unlooked-for Prince*), set in a Polynesian atmosphere, and has all the best tropes—arranged marriage, enemies-to-lovers, and more!

The Dream Trials is a novelette retelling of a Dutch fairy tale (*The Princess and the Pea*). After being caught in an enchanted rainfall following the queen's passing, Maribel's nights are plagued with strange dreams, her days full of pain and mystery—all preparing her for something she never could have imagined.

More information on JHouserWrites.com!